BY CHARLES BUKOWSKI

Flower, Fist and Bestial Wail (1960)
Poems and Drawings (1962)
Longshot Pomes for Broke Players (1962)
Run with the Hunted (1962)
It Catches My Heart in Its Hands (1963)
Crucifix in a Deathhand (1965)
Cold Dogs in the Courtyard (1965)
Confessions of a Man Insane Enough to Live with Beasts
     (1965)
The Genius of the Crowd (1966)
All the Assholes in the World and Mine (1966)
2 by Bukowski (1967)
The Curtains Are Waving (1967)
At Terror Street and Agony Way (1968)
Poems Written Before Jumping Out of an 8 Story
     Window (1968)
Notes of a Dirty Old Man (1969)
A Bukowski Sampler (1969)
The Days Run Away Like Wild Horses Over the Hills
     (1969)
Fire Station (1970)
Post Office (1971)
Mockingbird Wish Me Luck (1972)
Erections, Ejaculations, Exhibitions and General Tales
     of Ordinary Madness (1972)
Me and Your Sometimes Love Poems (1972)
While the Music Played (1973)
South of No North (1973)
Burning in Water, Drowning in Flame (1974)
Africa, Paris, Greece (1975)
Factotum (1975)
Scarlet (1976)
Maybe Tomorrow (1977)
Love is a Dog from Hell (1977)
You Kissed Lilly (1978)
We'll Take Them (1978)
Women (1978)
Play the Piano (1979)

LOVE IS A
DOG FROM
HELL / CHARLES
BUKOWSKI

Poems 1974-1977

SANTA BARBARA
BLACK SPARROW PRESS
1981

Grateful acknowledgement is made to the following publications where some of these poems first appeared: *Los Angeles Free Press, Poetry Now, Second Coming,* and *Wormwood Review.*

LIBRARY OF CONGRESS CATALOGING IN PUBLICATION DATA

Bukowski, Charles.
  Love is a dog from hell.

  I. Title.
PS3552.U4L6   811'.5'4   77-10501
ISBN 0-87685-363-7
ISBN 0-87685-362-9 pbk.

Sixth Printing

to Carl Weissner

table of contents

O N E

T H R E E

FOUR

1

one more creature
dizzy with love

Sandra

is the slim tall
ear-ringed
bedroom damsel
dressed in a long
gown

she's always high
in heels
spirit
pills
booze

Sandra leans out of
her chair
leans toward
Glendale

I wait for her head
to hit the closet
doorknob
as she attempts to
light
a new cigarette on an
almost burnt-out
one

at 32 she likes
young neat
unscratched boys
with faces like the bottoms
of new saucers

she has proclaimed as much
to me
has brought her prizes

over for me to view:
silent blonde zeros of young
flesh
who
a) sit
b) stand
c) talk
at her command

sometimes she brings one
sometimes two
sometimes three
for me to
view

Sandra looks very good in
long gowns
Sandra could probably break
a man's heart

I hope she finds
one.

you

you're a beast, she said
your big white belly
and those hairy feet.
you never cut your nails
and you have fat hands
paws like a cat
your bright red nose
and the biggest balls
I've ever seen.
you shoot sperm like a
whale shoots water out of the
hole in its back.

beast beast beast,
she kissed me,
what do you want for
breakfast?

the 6 foot goddess

I'm big
I suppose that's why my women always seem
small
but this 6 foot goddess
who deals in real estate
and art
and flies from Texas
to see me
and I fly to Texas
to see her—
well, there's plenty of her to
grab hold of
and I grab hold of it
of her,
I yank her head back by the hair,
I'm real macho,
I suck on her upper lip
her cunt
her soul
I mount her and tell her,
"I'm going to shoot white hot
juice into you. I didn't fly all the
way to Galveston to play
chess."

later we lay locked like human vines
my left arm under her pillow
my right arm over her side
I grip both of her hands,
and my chest
belly
balls
cock
tangle into her
and through us

in the dark
pass rays
back and forth
back and forth
until I fall away
and we sleep.

she's wild
but kind
my 6 foot goddess
makes me laugh
the laughter of the mutilated
who still need
love,
and her blessed eyes
run deep into her head
like mountain springs
far in
and
cool and good.

she has saved me
from everything that is
not here.

I've seen too many glazed-eyed
bums sitting under a bridge
drinking cheap wine

you sit on the couch
with me
tonight
new woman.

have you seen the
animal-eater
documentaries?

they show death.

and now I wonder
which animal of
us will eat the
other first
physically and
last
spiritually?

we consume animals
and then one of us
consumes the other,
my love.

meanwhile
I'd prefer you go
first the first way

since if past performance
charts mean anything
I'll surely go
first the last
way.

sexpot

"you know," she said, "you were at
the bar so you didn't see
but I danced with this guy.
we danced and we danced
close.
but I didn't go home with him
because he knew I was with
you."

"thanks a bunch," I
said.

she was always thinking of sex.
she carried it around with her
like something in a paper
bag.
such energy.
she never forgot.
she stared at every man available
in morning cafes
over bacon and eggs
or later
over a noon sandwich or
a steak dinner.

"I've modeled myself after
Marilyn Monroe," she told
me.

"she's always running off
to some local disco to dance
with a baboon," a friend once told
me, "I'm amazed that you've
stood for it as long as you have."

she'd vanish at racetracks
then come back and say,
"three men offered to buy me
a drink."

or I'd lose her in the parking
lot and I'd look up and she'd
be walking along with a strange man.
"well, he came from this direction
and I came from that and we
kind of walked together. I
didn't want to hurt his
feelings."

she said that I was a very
jealous man.

one day she just
fell down
inside of her sexual organs
and vanished.

it was like an alarm clock
dropping into the
Grand Canyon.
it banged and rattled and
rang and rang
but I could no longer
see or hear it.

I'm feeling much better
now.
I've taken up tap-dancing
and I wear a black felt
hat pulled down low
over my right
eye.

sweet music

it beats love because there aren't any
wounds: in the morning
she turns on the radio, Brahms or Ives
or Stravinsky or Mozart. she boils the
eggs counting the seconds out loud: 56,
57, 58 . . . she peels the eggs, brings
them to me in bed. after breakfast it's
the same chair and listen to the class-
ical music. she's on her first glass of
scotch and her third cigarette. I tell
her I must go to the racetrack. she's
been here about 2 nights and 2 days. "when
will I see you again?" I ask. she
suggests that might be up to me. I
nod and Mozart plays.

numb your ass and your
brain and your heart—

I was coming off an affair that had gone badly.
frankly, I was sliding down into a pit
really feeling shitty and low
when I lucked into this lady with a large bed
covered with a jeweled canopy
plus
wine, champagne, smokes, pills and
color tv.
we stayed in bed and
drank wine, champagne, smoked, popped pills
by the dozens
as I (feeling shitty and low)
tried to get over this affair that had gone
bad.
I watched the tv trying to dull my senses,
but the thing that really helped
was this very long
(specially written for tv) drama about
spies—
American spies and Russian spies, and
they were all so clever and
cool—
even their children didn't know
their wives didn't know, and
in a way
they hardly knew—
and I found out about counter-spies, double-spies:
guys who worked both sides, and
then this one who was a double-spy turned
into a triple-spy, it
got nicely confusing—
I don't even think the guy who wrote the script
knew what was happening—
it went on for hours!

seaplanes rammed into icebergs,
a priest in Madison, Wisc. murdered his brother,
a block of ice was shipped in a casket to Peru
in lieu of the world's largest diamond, and
blondes walked in and out of rooms eating
creampuffs and walnuts;
the triple-spy turned into a
quadruple-spy and everybody loved
everybody
and it went on and on
and the hours passed and
it all finally vanished like a paperclip in a
bag of trash and I
reached over and flicked off the set and
slept well for the first time
in a week and a half.

one of the hottest

she wore a platinum blond wig
and her face was rouged and powdered
and she put the lipstick on
making a huge painted mouth
and her neck was wrinkled
but she still had the ass of a young girl
and the legs were good.
she wore blue panties and I got them off
raised her dress, and with the TV flickering
I took her standing up.
as we struggled around the room
(I'm fucking the grave, I thought, I'm
bringing the dead back to life, marvelous
so marvelous
like eating cold olives at 3 a.m.
with half the town on fire)
I came.

you boys can keep your virgins
give me hot old women in high heels
with asses that forgot to get old.

of course, you leave afterwards
or get very drunk
which is the same
thing.

we drank wine for hours and watched tv
and when we went to bed
to sleep it off
she left her teeth in all
night long.

ashes

I got his ashes, she said, and I took them
out to sea and I scattered his ashes and
they didn't even look like ashes
and
the urn was weighted with
green and blue pebbles . . .

he didn't leave you any of his
millions?

nothing, she said.

after having to eat all those breakfasts
and lunches and dinners with him? after
listening to all his bullshit?

he was a brilliant man.

you know what I mean.

anyhow, I got the ashes. and you fucked
my sisters.

I never fucked your sisters.

yes, you did.

I fucked one of them.

which one?

the lesbian, I said, she bought me dinner and drinks,
I had very little choice.

I'm going, she said.

don't forget your bottle.

she went in and got it.

there's so little to you, she said, that when you die and
they burn you they'll have to add almost all green and
blue pebbles.

all right, I said.

I'll see you in 6 months! she screamed and slammed the door.

well, I thought, I guess in order to get rid of her I'll have
to fuck her other sister. I walked into the bedroom and started
looking for phone numbers. all I remembered was that she
lived in San Mateo and had a very good
job.

fuck

she pulled her dress off
over her head
and I saw the panties
indented somewhat into the
crotch.

it's only human.
now we've got to do it.
I've got to do it
after all that bluff.
it's like a party—
two trapped
idiots.

under the sheets
after I have snapped
off the light
her panties are still
on. she expects an
opening performance.
I can't blame her. but
wonder why she's here with
me? where are the other
guys? how can you be
lucky? having someone the
others have abandoned?

we didn't have to do it
yet we had to do it.
it was something like
establishing new credibility
with the income tax
man. I get the panties
off. I decide not to
tongue her. even then

I'm thinking about
after it's over.

we'll sleep together
tonight
trying to fit ourselves
inside the wallpaper.

I try, fail,
notice the hair on her
head
mostly notice the hair
on her
head
and a glimpse of
nostrils
piglike

I try it
again.

me

women don't know how to love,
she told me.
you know how to love
but women just want to
leech.
I know this because I'm a
woman.

hahaha, I laughed.

so don't worry about your breakup
with Susan
because she'll just leech onto
somebody else.

we talked a while longer
then I said goodbye
hungup
went into the crapper and
took a good beershit
mainly thinking, well,
I'm still alive
and have the ability to expell
wastes from my body.
and poems.
and as long as that's happening
I have the ability to handle
betrayal
loneliness
hangnail
clap
and the economic reports in the
financial section.

with that

I stood up
wiped
flushed
then thought:
it's true:
I know how to
love.

I pulled up my pants and walked
into the other room.

another bed

another bed
another woman

more curtains
another bathroom
another kitchen

other eyes
other hair
other
feet and toes.

everybody's looking.
the eternal search.

you stay in bed
she gets dressed for work
and you wonder what happened
to the last one
and the one before that . . .
it's all so comfortable—
this love-making
this sleeping together
the gentle kindness . . .

after she leaves you get up and use her
bathroom,
it's all so intimate and so strange.
you go back to bed and
sleep another hour.

when you leave it's with sadness
but you'll see her again
whether it works or not.

you drive down to the shore and sit
in your car. it's almost noon.

—another bed, other ears, other
ear rings, other mouths, other slippers, other
dresses
        colors, doors, phone numbers.

you were once strong enough to live alone.
for a man nearing sixty you should be more
sensible.

you start the car and shift,
thinking, I'll phone Jeanie when I get in,
I haven't seen her since Friday.

trapped

don't undress my love
you might find a mannequin;
don't undress the mannequin
you might find
my love.

she's long ago
forgotten me.

she's trying on a new
hat
and looks more the
coquette
than ever.

she is a
child
and a mannequin
and
death.

I can't hate
that.

she didn't do
anything
unusual.

I only wanted her
to.

tonight

"your poems about the girls will still be around
50 years from now when the girls are gone,"
my editor phones me.

dear editor:
the girls appear to be gone
already.

I know what you mean

but give me one truly alive woman
tonight
walking across the floor toward me

and you can have all the poems

the good ones
the bad ones
or any that I might write
after this one.

I know what you mean.

do you know what I mean?

the escape

escape from the black widow spider
is a miracle as great as art.
what a web she can weave
slowly drawing you to her
she'll embrace you
then when she's satisfied
she'll kill you
still in her embrace
and suck the blood from you.

I escaped my black widow
because she had too many males
in her web
and while she was embracing one
and then the other and then
another
I worked free
got out
to where I was before.

she'll miss me—
not my love
but the taste of my blood,
but she's good, she'll find other
blood;
she's so good that I almost miss my death,
but not quite;
I've escaped. I view the other
webs.

the drill

our marriage book, it
says.
I look through it.
they lasted ten years.
they were young once.
now I sleep in her bed.
he phones her:
"I want my drill back.
have it ready.
I'll pick the children up at
ten."
when he arrives he waits outside
the door.
his children leave with
him.
she comes back to bed
and I stretch a leg out
place it against hers.
I was young once too.
human relationships simply aren't
durable.
I think back to the women in
my life.
they seem non-existent.

"did he get his drill?" I ask.

"yes, he got his drill."

I wonder if I'll ever have to come
back for my bermuda
shorts and my record album
by The Academy of St. Martin in the
Fields? I suppose I
will.

texan

she's from Texas and weighs
103 pounds
and stands before the
mirror combing oceans
of reddish hair
which falls all the way down
her back to her ass.
the hair is magic and shoots
sparks as I lay on the bed
and watch her combing her
hair. she's like something
out of the movies but she's
actually here. we make love
at least once a day and
she can make me laugh
any time she cares
to. Texas women are always
healthy, and besides that she's
cleaned my refrigerator, my sink,
the bathroom, and she cooks and
feeds me healthy foods
and washes the dishes
too.

"Hank," she told me,
holding up a can of grapefruit
juice, "this is the best of them
all."
it says: Texas unsweetened
PINK grapefruit juice.

she looks like Katherine Hepburn
looked when she was
in high school, and I watch those
103 pounds

combing a yard and some change
of reddish hair
before the mirror
and I feel her inside of my
wrists and at the backs of my eyes,
and the toes and legs and belly
of me feel her and
the other part too,
and all of Los Angeles falls down
and weeps for joy,
the walls of the love parlors shake—
the ocean rushes in and she turns
to me and says, "damn this hair!"
and I say,
"yes."

the spider

then there was the time in
New Orleans
I was living with a fat woman,
Marie, in the French Quarter
and I got very sick.
while she was at work
I got down on my knees
in the kitchen
that afternoon and
prayed. I was not a
religious man
but it was a very dark afternoon
and I prayed:
"Dear God: if you will let me live,
I promise You I'll never take
another drink."
I kneeled there and it was just like
a movie—
as I finished praying
the clouds parted and the sun came
through the curtains
and fell upon me.
then I got up and took a crap.
there was a big spider in Marie's bathroom
but I crapped anyhow.
an hour later I began feeling much
better. I took a walk around the Quarter
and smiled at people.
I stopped at the grocery and got a couple of
6 packs for Marie.
I began feeling so good that an hour later
I sat in the kitchen and opened
one of the beers.
I drank that and then another one
and then I went in and

killed the spider.
when Marie got home from work
I gave her a big kiss,
then sat in the kitchen and talked
as she cooked dinner.
she asked me what had happened that day
and I told her I had killed the
spider. she didn't get
angry. she was a good
sort.

I tried it standing up
this time.
it doesn't usually
work.
this time it seemed
to . . .

she kept saying
"o my God, you've got
beautiful legs!"

it was all right
until she took her feet
off the ground
and wrapped her legs
around my middle.

"o my God, you've got
beautiful legs!"

she weighed about 138
pounds and hung there as I
worked.

it was when I climaxed
that I felt the pain
fly straight up my
spine.

I dropped her on the
couch and walked around
the room.
the pain remained.

"look," I told her,
"you better go. I've got

to develop some film
in my dark room."

she dressed and left
and I walked into the
kitchen for a glass of
water. I got a glass full
in my left hand.
the pain ran up behind my
ears and
I dropped the glass
which broke on the floor.

I got into a tub full of
hot water and epsom salts.
I just got stretched out
when the phone rang.
as I tried to straighten
my back
the pain extended to my
neck and arms.
I flopped about
gripped the sides of the tub
got out
with shots of green and yellow
and red light
flashing in my head.

the phone kept ringing.
I picked it up.
"hello?"

"I LOVE YOU!" she said.

"thanks," I said.

"is that all you've got
to say?"

"yes."

"eat shit!" she said and
hung up.

love dries up, I thought
as I walked back to the
bathroom, even faster
than sperm.

moaning and groaning

she writes: you'll
be moaning and groan-
ing in your poems
about how I fucked
those 2 guys last week.
I know you.
she writes on to
say that my vibe
machine was right—
she had just fucked
a third guy
but she knows I don't
want to hear who, why
or how. she closes her
letter, "Love."

rats and roaches
have triumphed again.
here it comes running
with a slug in its
mouth, it's singing
old love songs.
close the windows
moan
close the doors
groan.

an almost made up poem

I see you drinking at a fountain with tiny
blue hands, no, your hands are not tiny
they are small, and the fountain is in France
where you wrote me that last letter and
I answered and never heard from you again.
you used to write insane poems about
ANGELS AND GOD, all in upper case, and you
knew famous artists and most of them
were your lovers, and I wrote back, it's all right,
go ahead, enter their lives, I'm not jealous
because we've never met. we got close once in
New Orleans, one half block, but never met, never
touched. so you went with the famous and wrote
about the famous, and, of course, what you found out
is that the famous are worried about
their fame—not the beautiful young girl in bed
with them, who gives them *that,* and then awakens
in the morning to write upper case poems about
ANGELS AND GOD. we know God is dead, they've told
us, but listening to you I wasn't sure. maybe
it was the upper case. you were one of the
best female poets and I told the publishers,
editors, "print her, print her, she's mad but she's
magic. there's no lie in her fire." I loved you
like a man loves a woman he never touches, only
writes to, keeps little photographs of. I would have
loved you more if I had sat in a small room rolling a
cigarette and listened to you piss in the bathroom,
but that didn't happen. your letters got sadder.
your lovers betrayed you. kid, I wrote back, all
lovers betray. it didn't help. you said
you had a crying bench and it was by a bridge and
the bridge was over a river and you sat on the crying
bench every night and wept for the lovers who had
hurt and forgotten you. I wrote back but never

heard again. a friend wrote me of your suicide
3 or 4 months after it happened. if I had met you
I would probably have been unfair to you or you
to me. it was best like this.

blue cheese and chili peppers

these women are supposed to come
and see me
but they never
do.
there's the one with the long scar along her
belly.
there's the other who writes poems
and phones at 3 a.m., saying,
"I love you."
there's the one who dances with a
boa constrictor
and writes every four
weeks, she'll
come, she says.
and the 4th who claims she sleeps
always
with my latest book
under her
pillow.

I whack-off in the heat
and listen to Brahms and eat
blue cheese with chili
peppers.

these are women of good mind and
body, excellent in or out of bed,
dangerous and deadly, of
course—
but why do they all have to live
up north?

I know that someday they'll
arrive, but two or three
on the same day, and

we'll sit around and talk
and then they'll all leave
together.

somebody else will have them
and I will walk about
in my floppy shorts
smoking too many cigarettes
and trying to make drama
out of
no damned progress
at all.

problems about the other woman

I had worked my charms on her
for a couple of nights in a bar—
not that we were new lovers,
I had loved her for 16 months
but she didn't want to come to my place
"because that other woman has been there,"
and I said, "all right, all right, what will we do?"

she had come in from the north and was looking for a
place to stay
meanwhile rooming with her girlfriend,
and she went to her rent-a-trailer
and got out some blankets and said,
"let's go to the park."
I told her she was crazy
the cops would get us
but she said, "no, it's nice and foggy,"
so we went to the park
spread out the equipment and began
working and here came headlights—
a squad car—
she said, "hurry, get your pants on! I've got mine
on!"
I said, "I can't. they're all twisted-up."
and they came with flashlights
and asked what we were doing and she said,
"kissing!" one of the cops looked at me and
said, "I don't blame you," and after some small
talk they left us alone.
but she still didn't want the bed where that woman
had been,
so we ended up in a dark hot motel room
sweating and kissing and working
but we made it all right; but I mean,
after all that suffering . . .

we were at my place finally
that next afternoon
doing the same thing.

those weren't bad cops though
that night in the park—
and it's the first time I ever said that
about cops,
and,
I hope,
the last time I ever have
to.

T.M.

she lived in Galveston and was into
T.M.
and I went down to visit her and we made love
continually even though it was very warm
weather
and we took mescalin
and we took the ferry to the island
and drove 200 miles to the nearest
racetrack.
we both won and sat in a redneck bar—
disliked and distrusted by the natives—
and then we went to a redneck motel
and came back a day or two later
and I stayed another week
painted her a couple of good paintings—
one of a man being hanged
and another of a woman being fucked by a wolf.
I awakened one night and she wasn't in bed
and I got up and walked around saying,
"Gloria, Gloria, where are you?"
it was a large place and I walked around
opening door after door,
and then I opened what looked like a closet door
and there she was on her knees
surrounded by photographs of
7 or 8 men
heads shaved
most of them wearing rimless spectacles.
there was a small candle burning
and I said, "oh, I'm sorry."
Gloria was dressed in a kimono with flying
eagles on the back of it.
I closed the door and went back to bed.
she came out in 15 minutes.
we began kissing,
her large tongue sliding in and out of my

mouth.
she was a large healthy Texas girl.
"listen, Gloria," I finally managed to say,
"I need a night off."

the next day she drove me to the airport.
I promised to write. she promised to write.
neither of us has written.

Bee's 5th

I heard it first while screwing a blonde
who had the biggest box in
Scranton.

I listened to it again as I wrote a letter
to my mother
asking for 5,000 dollars
and she mailed back
3 bottletops and
the stems of grandpop's
forefingers.

The 5th will kill you
in the grass or at the track,
the kitten said,
walking across the popinjay
rug.

if the 5th don't kill you
the tenth will,
said the Caliente hooker.
as they ran up the
beautiful catsup red flag
93 thieves wept in the
purple dust.

the 5th is like an
ant in a breakfastnook full of
swaggersticks and
june bugs
sucking
dawn's orange juice coming.

and I took the 3 bottletops from my
mother and

ate them
wrapped in pages from
Cosmopolitan
magazine.

but I *am* tired of the
5th
and I told this to a woman in
Ohio once, I
had just packed coal up 3 flights
of stairs
I was drunk and
dizzy, and she said:

> how can you say you don't care
> for something greater than you'll
> ever be?

and I said:

> that's easy.

and she sat in a green chair and
I sat in a red chair
and after that
we never made love
again.

103 degrees

she cut my toenails the night before,
and in the morning she said, "I think I'll
just lay here all day."
which meant she wasn't going to work.
she was at my apartment—which meant another
day and another night.
she was a good person
but she had just told me that she wanted to
have a child, wanted marriage, and
it was 103 degrees outside.
when I thought of *another* child and
another marriage
I really began to feel bad.
I had resigned myself to dying alone
in a small room—
now she was trying to reshape my master plan.
besides she always slammed my car door too loud
and ate with her head too close to the table.
this day we had gone to the post office, a department
store and then to a sandwich place for lunch.
I already felt married. driving back in I almost
ran into a Cadillac.
"let's get drunk," I said.
"no, no," she answered, "it's too early."
and then she slammed the car door.
it was still 103 degrees.
when I opened my mail I found my auto insurance
company wanted $76 more.
suddenly she ran into the room and screamed, "LOOK, I'M
TURNING RED! ALL BLOTCHY! WHAT'LL I DO!"
"take a bath," I told her.
I dialed the insurance company long distance and
demanded to know why.
she began screaming and moaning from the
bathtub and I couldn't hear and I said, "just a

moment, please!"
I covered the phone and screamed at her in the bathtub:
"LOOK! I'M ON LONG DISTANCE! HOLD IT DOWN, FOR CHRIST'S
SAKE!"
the insurance people still maintained that I owed them
$76 and would send me a letter explaining why.
I hung up and stretched out on the bed.
I was already married, I felt married.
she came out of the bathroom and said, "can I stretch out
beside you?"
and I said, "o.k."
in ten minutes her color was normal.
it was because she had taken a niacin tablet.
she remembered that it happened every time.
we stretched out there sweating:
nerves. nobody has soul enough to overcome nerves.
but I couldn't tell her that.
she wanted her baby.
what the fuck.

you go for these wenches, she said,
you go for these whores,
I'll bore you.

I don't want to be shit on anymore,
I said,
relax.

when I drink, she said, it hurts my
bladder, it burns.

I'll do the drinking, I said.

you're waiting for the phone to ring,
she said,
you keep looking at the phone.
if one of those wenches phones you'll
run right out of here.

I can't promise you anything, I said.

then—just like that—the phone rang.

this is Madge, said the phone. I've
got to see you right away.

oh, I said.

I'm in a jam, she continued, I need ten
bucks—fast.

I'll be right over, I said, and
hung up.

she looked at me. it was a wench,
she said, your whole face lit up.

what the hell's the matter with
you?

listen, I said, I've got to leave.
you stay here. I'll be right back.

I'm going, she said. I love you but you're
crazy, you're doomed.

she got her purse and slammed the door.

it's probably some deeply-rooted childhood fuckup
that makes me vulnerable, I thought.

then I left my place and got into my volks.
I drove north up Western with the radio on.
there were whores walking up and down
both sides of the street and Madge looked
more vicious than any of them.

225 pounds

we were in bed and
she started to fight:
"you son of a bitch! you just wait a minute,
I'll get you!"

I began laughing:
"what's the matter? what's the matter?"

"you son of a bitch!" she screamed.

I held her hands as she squirmed.

she was a couple of decades younger than I
a health food freak.
she was *very* strong.

"you son of a bitch! I'll get you!"
she screamed.

I rolled on top of her with my 225 pounds and
just layed it there on her.

"uugg, oooo, my God, that's not *fair*, oooo, my
God!"

I rolled off and walked into the other room and
sat on the couch.

"I'll get you, bastard," she said, "you just
wait!"

"just don't bite it off," I said, "or you'll make
a half dozen women very unhappy."

she climbed up on the headboard of my bed
(it did have a flat though narrow surface)

and sat perched there watching the news on
tv.
the tv faced the bedroom and it illuminated
her as she sat up there on the
headboard.

"I thought you were sane," I said, "but you're
just as crazy as the rest of them."

"be quiet," she said, "I want to watch the
news!"

"look," I said, "I'll . . ."

"SHUSH!" she said.

and there she was up on the headboard of my bed
really watching the news. I accepted her that
way.

turnabout

she drives into the parking lot while
I am leaning up against the fender of my car.
she's drunk and her eyes are wet with tears:
"you son of a bitch, you fucked me when you
didn't want to. you told me to keep phoning
you, you told me to move closer into town,
then you told me to leave you alone."

it's all quite dramatic and I enjoy it.
"sure, well, what do you want?"

"I want to talk to you, I want to go to your
place and talk to you . . ."

"I'm with somebody now. she's in getting a
sandwich."

"I want to talk to you . . . it takes a while
to get over things. I need more time."

"sure. wait until she comes out. we're not
inhuman. we'll all have a drink together."

"shit," she says, "oh shit!"

she jumps into her car and drives off.

the other one comes out: "who was that?"

"an ex-friend."

now *she's* gone and I'm sitting here drunk
and my eyes seem wet with tears.

it's very quiet and I feel like I have a spear
rammed into the center of my gut.

I walk to the bathroom and puke.

mercy, I think, doesn't the human race know anything
about mercy?

one for old snaggle-tooth

I know a woman
who keeps buying puzzles
chinese
puzzles
blocks
wires
pieces that finally fit
into some order.
she works it out
mathematically
she solves all her
puzzles
lives down by the sea
puts sugar out for the ants
and believes
ultimately
in a better world.
her hair is white
she seldom combs it
her teeth are snaggled
and she wears loose shapeless
coveralls over a body most
women would wish they had.
for many years she irritated me
with what I considered her
eccentricities—
like soaking eggshells in water
(to feed the plants so that
they'd get calcium).
but finally when I think of her
life
and compare it to other lives
more dazzling, original
and beautiful
I realize that she has hurt fewer

people than anybody I know
(and by hurt I simply mean hurt).
she has had some terrible times,
times when maybe I should have
helped her more
for she is the mother of my only
child
and we were once great lovers,
but she has come through
like I said
she has hurt fewer people than
anybody I know,
and if you look at it like that,
well,
she has created a better world.
she has won.

Frances, this poem is for
you.

communion

horses running
with her miles away
laughing with a
fool

Bach and the hydrogen bomb
and her miles away
laughing with a
fool

the banking system
bumper jacks
gondolas in Venice
and her miles away
laughing with a
fool

you've never quite
seen a stairway before
(each step looking at you
separately)
and outside
the newsboy looking
immortal
as the cars go by
under a sun
like an enemy
and you wonder
why it's so hard
to go crazy—
if you're not already
crazy

until now
you've never seen a

stairway that looked like
a stairway
a doorknob that looked like
a doorknob
and sounds like these sounds

and when the spider comes out
and looks at you
finally
you don't hate it
finally
with her miles away
laughing with a
fool.

trying to get even:

we'd had any number of joints and some
beer and I was on the bed stretched out
and she said, "look, I've had 3 abortions
in a row, real fast, and I'm sick of
abortions, I don't want you to stick that
thing in me!"

it was sticking up there and we were both
looking at it.
"ah, come on," I said, "my girlfriend fucked
2 different guys this week and I'm trying to
get even."

"don't get me involved in your domestic
horseshit! now what I want you to do is
to BEAT that thing OFF while I WATCH!
I want to WATCH while you beat that thing
OFF! I want to see it shoot JUICE!"

"o.k. get your face closer."

she got it closer and I spit on my palm
and began working.

it got bigger. just before I was ready I
stopped, I held it at the bottom
stretching it,
the head throbbed
purple and shiny.

"oooh," she said.
she ducked her mouth over it, sucked at
it and
pulled away.

"finish it off," I said.

69

"no!"

I whacked away and then stopped again
at the last moment and held it at the
bottom and waved it all around the
bedroom.

she eyed it
fell upon it again
sucked
and pulled away.

we alternated the process
back and forth

again and again.

finally I just pulled her off
the chair
onto the bed
rolled on top of her
stuck it in
worked it
worked it
and came.

when she walked back out of
the bathroom she said,
"you son of a bitch, I love you,
I've loved you for a long time.
when I get back to Santa Barbara
I'm going to write you. I'm
living with this guy but I hate
him, I don't even know what I'm
doing with him."

"o.k.," I said, "but you're up
now. can you get me a glass of
water? I'm dry."

she walked into the kitchen and
I heard her remark that
all my drinking glasses were
dirty.

I told her to use a
coffee cup. I
heard the water running and I
thought, one more fuck
I'll be even
and I can be in love with my girlfriend again—
that is
if she hasn't slipped in an
extra
and she probably
has.

Chicago

"I've made it," she said, "I've come
through." she had on new boots, pants
and a white sweater. "I know what I
want now." she was from Chicago and
had settled in L.A.'s Fairfax district.

"you promised me champagne,"
she said.
"I was drunk when I phoned. how about
a beer?"
"no, pass me your joint."
she inhaled, let it out:
"this isn't very good stuff."
she handed it back.

"there's a difference," I said, "between
making it and simply becoming hard."

"you like my boots?"
"yes, very nice."
"listen, I've got to go. can I use
your bathroom?"
"sure."

when she came out she had on a
large lipstick mouth. I hadn't seen
one of those since I was a boy.
I kissed her in the doorway
feeling the lipstick rub off on my
lips.

"goodbye," she said.
"goodbye," I said.

she went up the walk toward her car.
I closed the door.

she knew what she wanted and it wasn't
me.
I know more women like that than any
other kind.

quiet clean girls in gingham dresses . . .

all I've ever known are whores, ex-prostitutes,
madwomen. I see men with quiet,
gentle women—I see them in the supermarkets,
I see them walking down the streets together,
I see them in their apartments: people at
peace, living together. I know that their
peace is only partial, but there is
peace, often hours and days of peace.

all I've ever known are pill freaks, alcoholics,
whores, ex-prostitutes, madwomen.

when one leaves
another arrives
worse than her predecessor.

I see so many men with quiet clean girls in
gingham dresses
girls with faces that are not wolverine or
predatory.

"don't ever bring a whore around," I tell my
few friends, "I'll fall in love with her."

"you couldn't stand a good woman, Bukowski."

I need a good woman. I need a good woman
more than I need this typewriter, more than
I need my automobile, more than I need
Mozart; I need a good woman so badly that I
can taste her in the air, I can feel her
at my fingertips, I can see sidewalks built
for her feet to walk upon,
I can see pillows for her head,
I can feel my waiting laughter,

I can see her petting a cat,
I can see her sleeping,
I can see her slippers on the floor.

I know that she exists
but where is she upon this earth
as the whores keep finding me?

we will taste the islands
and the sea

I know that some night
in some bedroom
soon
my fingers will
rift
through
soft clean
hair

songs such as no radio
plays

all sadness, grinning
into flow.

2

me, and
that old woman:
sorrow

this
poet

this poet he'
d been drink
ing 2 or 3 da
ys and he wa
lked out on t
he stage and
looked at th
at   audience
and he just k
new he was
going to do i
t. there was
a grand pian
o on stage a
nd he walke
d over and li
fted the lid a
nd vomited i
nside the pia
no. then he c
losed the lid
and gave his
reading.

they had to r
emove the st
rings from t
he piano and
wash out the
insides and r
estring it.

I can unders

tand why th
ey never invi
ted him bac
k. but to pas
s the word o
n to other un
iversities tha
t he was a
poet who lik
ed to vomit i
nto grand pi
anos was un
fair.

they never c
onsidered th
e quality of
his reading.
I know this
poet: he's ju
st like the re
st of us: he'l
l vomit anyw
here for mon
ey.

big sloppy wounded dog
hit by a car and walking
toward the curbing
making enormous
sounds
your body curled
red blowing out of
ass and mouth.

I stare at him and
drive on
for how would it look
for me to be holding
a dying dog on a
curbing in Arcadia,
blood seeping into my
shirt and pants and
shorts and socks and
shoes? it would just
look dumb.
besides, I figure the 2
horse in the first race
and I wanted to hook
him with the 9
in the second. I
figured the daily to
pay around $140
so I had to let that
dog die alone there
just across from the
shopping center
with the ladies look-
ing for bargains
as the first bit of
snow fell upon the
Sierra Madre.

what they want

Vallejo writing about
loneliness while starving to
death;
Van Gogh's ear rejected by a
whore;
Rimbaud running off to Africa
to look for gold and finding
an incurable case of syphilis;
Beethoven gone deaf;
Pound dragged through the streets
in a cage;
Chatterton taking rat poison;
Hemingway's brains dropping into
the orange juice;
Pascal cutting his wrists
in the bathtub;
Artaud locked up with the mad;
Dostoevsky stood up against a wall;
Crane jumping into a boat propeller;
Lorca shot in the road by Spanish
troops;
Berryman jumping off a bridge;
Burroughs shooting his wife;
Mailer knifing his.
—that's what they want:
a God damned show
a lit billboard
in the middle of hell.
that's what they want,
that bunch of
dull
inarticulate
safe
dreary
admirers of
carnivals.

Iron Mike

we talk about this film:
Cagney fed this broad
grapefruit
faster than she could
eat it and
then she
loved him.

"that won't always
work," I told Iron
Mike.

he grinned and said,
"yeh."

then he reached down
and touched his belt.
32 female scalps
dangled there.

"me and my big Jewish
cock," he said.

then he raised his hands
to indicate the
size.

"o, yeh, well,"
I said.

"they come around," he
said, "I fuck 'em, they
hang around, I tell 'em,
'it's time to leave.' "

"you've got guts,
Mike."

"this one wouldn't leave
so I just got up and
slapped her . . . she
left."

"I don't have your nerve,
Mike. they hang around
washing dishes, rubbing
the shit-stains out of the
crapper, throwing out the
old Racing Forms . . ."

"they'll never get me,"
he said,
"I'm invincible."

look, Mike, no man is
invincible.
some day
you'll be sent mad by
eyes like a child's crayon
drawing. you won't be
able to drink a glass of
water or walk across a
room. there will be the
walls and the sound of
the streets outside, and
you'll hear machineguns
and mortar shells. that'll
be when you want it and
can't have it.

the teeth
are never finally the
teeth of love.

guru

big black beard
tells me
that I don't feel
terror

I look at him
my gut rattles
gravel

I see his eyes
look upward

he's strong

has dirty fingernails

and upon the walls:
scabbards.

he knows things:

books
the odds
the best road
home

I like him
but I think he
lies

(I'm not sure
he lies)

his wife sits
in a dark

corner

when I first met
her she was the
most beautiful
woman
I had ever
seen

now she has
become
his twin

perhaps not his
fault:

perhaps the thing
does us all
like that

yet after I leave
their house
I feel terror

the moon looks
diseased

my hands slip
on the
steering wheel

I get my car
out
and down the
hill

almost crash it
into a
blue-green
parked car

clod me forever,
Beatrice

wavering poet, ha
haha

dinky dog of
terror.

the professors

sitting with the professors
we talk about Allen Tate
and John Crow Ransom
the rugs are clean and
the coffeetables shine
and there is talk of
budgets and works in
progress
and there is a
fireplace.
the kitchen floor is
well-waxed
and I have just eaten
dinner
after drinking until
3 a.m.
after reading
the night before

now I'm to read again
at a nearby college.
I'm in Arkansas in
January
somebody even mentions
Faulkner
I go to the bathroom
and vomit up the
dinner
when I come out
they are all in their
coats and overcoats
waiting in the
kitchen.
I'm to read in
15 minutes.

there'll be a
good crowd
they tell me.

for Al—

don't worry about rejections, pard,
I've been rejected
before.

sometimes you make a mistake, taking
the wrong poem
more often I make the mistake, writing
it.

but I like a mount in every race
even though the man
who puts up the morning line

tabs it 30 to one.

I get to thinking about death more and
more

senility

crutches

armchairs

writing purple poetry with a
dripping pen

when the young girls with mouths
like barracudas
bodies like lemon trees
bodies like clouds
bodies like flashes of lightning
stop knocking on my door.

don't worry about rejections, pard.

I have smoked 25 cigarettes tonight
and you know about the beer.

the phone has only rung once:
wrong number.

how to be a great writer

you've got to fuck a great many women
beautiful women
and write a few decent love poems.

and don't worry about age
and/or freshly-arrived talents.

just drink more beer
more and more beer

and attend the racetrack at least once a
week

and win
if possible.

learning to win is hard—
any slob can be a good loser.

and don't forget your Brahms
and your Bach and your
beer.

don't overexercise.

sleep until noon.

avoid credit cards
or paying for anything on
time.

remember that there isn't a piece of ass
in this world worth over $50
(in 1977).

and if you have the ability to love
love yourself first
but always be aware of the possibility of
total defeat
whether the reason for that defeat
seems right or wrong—

an early taste of death is not necessarily
a bad thing.

stay out of churches and bars and museums,
and like the spider be
patient—
time is everybody's cross,
plus
exile
defeat
treachery

all that dross.

stay with the beer.

beer is continous blood.

a continuous lover.

get a large typewriter
and as the footsteps go up and down
outside your window

hit that thing
hit it hard

make it a heavyweight fight

make it the bull when he first charges in

and remember the old dogs
who fought so well:
Hemingway, Celine, Dostoevsky, Hamsun.

if you think they didn't go crazy
in tiny rooms
just like you're doing now

without women
without food
without hope

then you're not ready.

drink more beer.
there's time.
and if there's not
that's all right
too.

the price

drinking 15 dollar champagne—
Cordon Rouge—with the hookers.

one is named Georgia and she
doesn't like pantyhose:
I keep helping her pull up
her long dark stockings.

the other is Pam—prettier
but not much soul, and
we smoke and talk and I
play with their legs and
stick my bare foot into
Georgia's open purse.
it's filled with
bottles of pills. I
take some of the pills.

"listen," I say, "one of
you has soul, the other
looks. can't I combine
the 2 of you? take the soul
and stick it into the looks?"

"you want me," says Pam, "it
will cost you a hundred."

we drink some more and Georgia
falls to the floor and can't
get up.

I tell Pam that I like her
earrings very much. her
hair is long and a natural
red.

"I was only kidding about the
hundred," she says.

"oh," I say, "what will it cost
me?"

she lights her cigarette with
my lighter and looks at me
through the flame:

her eyes tell me.

"look," I say, "I don't think I
can ever pay that price again."

she crosses her legs
inhales on her cigarette

as she exhales she smiles
and says, "sure you can."

the flesh covers the bone
and they put a mind
in there and
sometimes a soul,
and the women break
vases against the walls
and the men drink too
much
and nobody finds the
one
but they keep
looking
crawling in and out
of beds.
flesh covers
the bone and the
flesh searches
for more than
flesh.

there's no chance
at all:
we are all trapped
by a singular
fate.

nobody ever finds
the one.

the city dumps fill
the junkyards fill
the madhouses fill
the hospitals fill
the graveyards fill

nothing else
fills.

the 2nd novel

they'd come around and
they'd ask
"you finished your
2nd novel yet?"

"no."

"whatsamatta? whatsamatta
that you can't
finish it?"

"hemorrhoids and
insomnia."

"maybe you've lost
it?"

"lost what?"

"you know."

now when they come
around I tell them,
"yeh. I finished
it. be out in Sept."

"you *finished* it?"

"yeh."

"well, listen, I gotta
go."

even the cat
here in the courtyard
won't come to my door
anymore.

it's nice.

Chopin Bukowski

this is my piano.

the phone rings and people ask,
what are you doing? how about
getting drunk with us?

and I say,
I'm at my piano.

what?

I'm at my piano.

I hang up.

people need me. I fill
them. if they can't see me
for a while they get desperate, they get
sick.

but if I see them too often
I get sick. it's hard to feed
without getting fed.

my piano says things back to
me.

sometimes the things are
scrambled and not very good.
other times
I get as good and lucky as
Chopin.

sometimes I get out of practice
out of tune. that's
all right.

I can sit down and vomit on the
keys
but it's my
vomit.

it's better than sitting in a room
with 3 or 4 people and
their pianos.

this is my piano
and it is better than theirs.

and they like it and they do not
like it.

gloomy lady

she sits up there
drinking wine
while her husband
is at work.
she puts quite
some importance
upon getting her
poems published
in the little
magazines.
she's had two or
three of her slim
volumes of poems
done in mimeo.
she has two or
three children
between the ages
of 6 and 15.
she is no longer
the beautiful woman
she was. she sends
photos of herself
sitting upon a rock
by the ocean
alone and damned.
I could have had
her once. I wonder
if she thinks I
could have
saved her?

in all her poems
her husband is
never mentioned.
but she does

talk about her
garden
so we know that's
there, anyhow,
and maybe she
fucks the rosebuds
and finches
before she writes
her poems

cockroach

the cockroach crouched
against the tile
while I was pissing and as
I turned my head
he hauled his butt
into a crack.
I got the can and sprayed
and sprayed and sprayed
and finally the roach came out
and gave me a very dirty look.
then he fell down into
the bathtub and I watched
him dying
with a subtle pleasure
because I paid the rent
and he didn't.
I picked him up with
some greenblue toilet
paper and flushed him
away. that's all there
was to that, except
around Hollywood and
Western we have to
keep doing it.
they say some day that
tribe is going to
inherit the earth
but we're going to
make them wait a
few months.

who in the hell is
Tom Jones?

I was shacked with a
24 year old girl from
New York City for
two weeks—about
the time of the garbage
strike out there, and
one night my 34 year
old woman arrived and
she said, "I want to see
my rival." she did
and then she said, "o,
you're a cute little thing!"
next I knew there was a
screech of wildcats—
such screaming and scratch-
ing, wounded animal moans,
blood and piss . . .

I was drunk and in my
shorts. I tried to
separate them and fell,
wrenched my knee. then
they were through the screen
door and down the walk
and out in the street.

squadcars full of cops
arrived. a police heli-
copter circled overhead.

I stood in the bathroom
and grinned in the mirror.
it's not often at the age
of 55 that such splendid

things occur.
better than the Watts
riots.

the 34 year old
came back in. she had
pissed all over her-
self and her clothing
was torn and she was
followed by 2 cops who
wanted to know why.

pulling up my shorts
I tried to explain.

defeat

listening to Bruckner on the radio
wondering why I'm not half mad
over the latest breakup with my
latest girlfriend

wondering why I'm not driving the streets
drunk
wondering why I'm not in the bedroom
in the dark
in the grievous dark
pondering
ripped by half-thoughts.

I suppose
that at last
like the average man:
I've known too many women
and instead of thinking,
I wonder who's fucking her now?
I think
she's giving some other poor son of a bitch
much trouble right now.

listening to Bruckner on the radio
seems so peaceful.

too many women have gone through.
I am at last alone
without being alone.

I pick up a Grumbacher paint brush
and clean my fingernails with the hard sharp end.

I notice a wall socket.

look, I've won.

traffic signals

the old folks play a game
in the park overlooking the sea
shoving markers across cement
with wooden sticks.
four play, two on each side
and 18 or 20 others sit in
the sun and watch
I notice this as I move
toward the public facility
as my car is being repaired.

an old cannon sits in the park
rusted and useless.
six or seven sailboats ride
the sea below.

I finish my duty
come out
and they are still playing.

one of the women is heavily rouged
wearing false eyelashes and smoking
a cigarette.
the men are very thin
very pale
wear wristwatches that hurt
their wrists.

the other woman is very fat
and giggles
each time a score is made

some of them are my age.

they disgust me
the way they wait for death

with as much passion
as a traffic signal.

these are the people who believe advertisements
these are the people who buy dentures on credit
these are the people who celebrate holidays
these are the people who have grandchildren
these are the people who vote
these are the people who have funerals

these are the dead
the smog
the stink in the air
the lepers.

these are almost everybody
finally.

seagulls are better
seaweed is better
dirty sand is better

if I could turn that old cannon
on them
and make it work
I would.

they disgust me.

462-0614

I get many phonecalls now.
They are all alike.
"are you Charles Bukowski,
the writer?"
"yes," I tell them.
and they tell me
that they understand my
writing,
and some of them are writers
or want to be writers
and they have dull and
horrible jobs
and they can't face the room
the apartment
the walls
that night—
they want somebody to talk
to,
and they can't believe
that I can't help them
that I don't know the words.
they can't believe
that often now
I double up in my room
grab my gut
and say
"Jesus Jesus Jesus, not
again!"
they can't believe
that the loveless people
the streets
the loneliness
the walls
are mine too.
and when I hang up the phone

111

they think I have held back my
secret.

I don't write out of
knowledge.
when the phone rings
I too would like to hear words
that might ease
some of this.

that's why my number's
listed.

photographs

they photograph you on your porch
and on your couch
and standing in the courtyard
or leaning against your car

these photographers
women with big asses
which look better to you
than do their eyes or their souls

—this playing at author
it's real Hemingway
James Joyce
stageshit

but look—
there are the books
you've written them
you haven't been to Paris
but you've written all those books
there behind you
(and others not there,
lost or stolen)

all you've got to do
is look like Bukowski
for the cameras
but

you keep watching
those
astonishingly big asses
and thinking—
somebody else is getting
it

"look into my eyes,"
they say and click their cameras
and flash their cameras
and fondle their cameras

Hemingway used to box or go
fishing or to the bullfights
but after they leave
you jerk-off into the sheets
and take a hot bath

they never send the photos
like they promise to send the photos
and the astonishingly big asses are
gone forever
and you've been a fine literary fellow—
now alive
dead soon enough
looking into and at their eyes and souls
and more.

social

the blue pencil of the wave
shots of yellow road

a steering wheel
an insane woman sitting
next to you

complaining as the ocean
creams-off

and people in yellow and
white
campers
block your way
a frantic
time
as you listen
guilty of this and
guilty of that

you admit
this and that
but it's not
enough

she wants splendid
conquest
and you're weary of
splendid
conquest

getting there
she climbs out
walks toward the
house

you piss across the
fender of your car
drunk on beer

little spots of you
dripping down into
the dust
the dry
dust

zipping up you
march in to
meet her
friends.

one to the breastplate

I have a saying, "the tough ones always come
back."

but Vera was kinder than most,
and so I was surprised when
she arrived that night
and said, "let me in."

"no, no, I'm working on a sonnet."

"I'll just stay a minute, then I'll
leave."

"Vera, if I let you in you'll be here
for 3 or 4 days."

it was night and I hadn't turned the
porch light on so I couldn't see it
coming
but
she threw a right that
exploded in the center of my
chest.

"baby, that was a beautiful punch.
now move off."

then I closed the door.

she was back again in 5 minutes:
"Hank, I can't find my car, I
swear I can't find my car. help
me find my car!"

I saw my friend Bobby-the-Riff

walking by. "hey, Bobby, help
this one find her car. we'll
even it up later."

they went off together.

later Bobby said they found her
car parked on somebody's front
lawn, lights on and motor
running.

I haven't heard from Vera
since
unless she's the one
who keeps phoning at
2 and 3 and 4 a.m. in the
morning
and doesn't answer when I
say "hello."

but Bobby says he
can handle her
so I've decided to turn her over
to Bobby.

she lives on a side street somewhere
in Glendale
and I help him unfold the
roadmap as we sip our
diet Schlitz.

the worst and the best

in the hospitals and jails
it's the worst
in madhouses
it's the worst
in penthouses
it's the worst
in skid row flophouses
it's the worst
at poetry readings
at rock concerts
at benefits for the disabled
it's the worst
at funerals
at weddings
it's the worst
at parades
at skating rinks
at sexual orgies
it's the worst
at midnight
at 3 a.m.
at 5:45 p.m.
it's the worst

falling through the sky
firing squads
that's the best

thinking of India
looking at popcorn stands
watching the bull get the matador
that's the best

boxed lightbulbs
an old dog scratching

119

peanuts in a celluloid bag
that's the best

spraying roaches
a clean pair of stockings
natural guts defeating natural talent
that's the best

in front of firing squads
throwing crusts to seagulls
slicing tomatoes
that's the best

rugs with cigarette burns
cracks in sidewalks
waitresses still sane
that's the best

my hands dead
my heart dead
silence
adagio of rocks
the world ablaze
that's the best
for me.

coupons

cigarettes wetted with beer from
the night before
you light one
gag
open the door for air
and on your doorstep
is a dead sparrow
his head and breast
chewed away.

hanging from the doorknob
is an ad from the All American
Burger
consisting of several coupons
which
say
that with the purchase
of a burger
from Feb. 12 thru Feb. 15
you can get a free
regular size bag of french
fries and one
10 oz. cup of coca cola.

I take the ad
wrap the sparrow
carry him to the trash bin
and dump him
in.

look:
forsaking fries and coke
to help keep
my city
clean.

luck

what's bad about all
this
is watching people
drinking coffee and
waiting. I would
douse them all
with luck. they need
it. they need it
worse than I do.

I sit in cafes
and watch them
waiting. I suppose
there's not much
else to do. the
flies walk up and
down the windows
and we drink our
coffee and pretend
not to look at
each other. I
wait with them.
between the move-
ment of the flies
people walk by.

dog

a single dog
walking alone on a hot sidewalk of
summer
appears to have the power
of ten thousand gods.

why is this?

trench warfare

sick with the flu
drinking beer
my radio on loud
enough to overcome
the sounds of the
stereo people who
have just moved
into the court
across the way.
asleep or awake
they play their
set at top volume
leaving their
doors and windows
open.

they are each
18, married, wear
red shoes,
are blonde,
slim.
they play
everything: jazz,
classical, rock,
country, modern
as long as it is
loud.

this is the problem
of being poor:
we must share each
other's sounds.
last week it was
my turn:
there were two women

in here
fighting each other
and then they
ran up the walk
screaming.
the police came.

now it's their
turn.
now I am walking
up and down in
my dirty shorts,
two rubber earplugs
stuck deep into
my ears.

I even consider
murder.
such rude little
rabbits!
walking little pieces
of snot!

but in our land
and in our way
there has never
been a chance;
it's only when
things are not
going too badly
for a while
that we forget.

someday they'll
each be dead
someday they'll
each have a
separate coffin
and it will be
quiet.

but right now
it's Bob Dylan
Bob Dylan Bob
Dylan all the
way.

the night I fucked my alarm clock

once
starving in Philadelphia
I had a small room
it was evening going into night
and I stood at my window on the 3rd floor
in the dark and looked down into a
kitchen across the way on the 2nd floor
and I saw a beautiful blonde girl
embrace a young man there and kiss him
with what seemed hunger
and I stood and watched until they broke
away.
then I turned and switched on the room light.
I saw my dresser and my dresser drawers
and my alarm clock on the dresser.
I took my alarm clock
to bed with me and
fucked it until the hands dropped off.
then I went out and walked the streets
until my feet blistered.
when I got back I walked to the window
and looked down and across the way
and the light in their kitchen was
out.

when I think of myself dead

I think of automobiles parked in a
parking lot

when I think of myself dead
I think of frying pans

when I think of myself dead
I think of somebody making love to you
when I'm not around

when I think of myself dead
I have trouble breathing

when I think of myself dead
I think of all the people waiting to die

when I think of myself dead
I think I won't be able to drink water anymore

when I think of myself dead
the air goes all white

the roaches in my kitchen
tremble

and somebody will have to throw
my clean and dirty underwear
away.

Christmas eve, alone

Christmas eve, alone,
in a motel room
down the coast
near the Pacific—
hear it?

they've tried to do this place up
Spanish, there's
tapestry and lamps, and
the toilet's clean, there are
tiny bars of pink
soap.

they won't find us
here:
the barracudas or the ladies or
the idol
worshippers.

back in town
they're drunk and panicked
running red lights
breaking their heads open
in honor of Christ's
birthday. that's nice.

soon I'll finish this 5th of
Puerto Rican rum.
in the morning I'll vomit and
shower, drive back
in, have a sandwich by 1 p.m.,
be back in my room by
2,
stretched on the bed,
waiting for the phone to ring,

not answering,
my holiday is an
evasion, my reasoning
is not.

there once was a woman who put her head into an oven

terror finally becomes almost
bearable
but never quite

terror creeps like a cat
crawls like a cat
across my mind

I can hear the laughter of the masses

they are strong
they will survive

like the roach

never take your eyes off the roach

you'll never see it again.

the masses are everywhere
they know how to do things:
they have sane and deadly angers
for sane and deadly
things.

I wish I were driving a blue 1952 Buick
or a dark blue 1942 Buick
or a blue 1932 Buick
over a cliff of hell and into the
sea.

beds, toilets, you and
me—

think of the beds
used again and again
to fuck in
to die in.

in this land
some of us fuck more than
we die
but most of us die
better than we
fuck,
and we die
piece by piece too—
in parks
eating ice cream, or
in igloos
of dementia,
or on straw mats
or upon disembarked
loves
or
or.

:beds beds beds
:toilets toilets toilets

the human sewage system
is the world's greatest
invention.

and you invented me
and I invented you
and that's why we don't
get along

on this bed
any longer.
you were the world's
greatest invention
until you
flushed me
away.

now it's your turn
to wait for the touch
of the handle.
somebody will do it
to you,
bitch,
and if they don't
you will—
mixed with your own
green or yellow or white
or blue
or lavender
goodbye.

this then—

it's the same as before
or the other time
or the time before that.
here's a cock
and here's a cunt
and here's trouble.

only each time
you think
well now I've learned:
I'll let her do that
and I'll do this,
I no longer want it all,
just some comfort
and some sex
and only a minor
love.

now I'm waiting again
and the years run thin.
I have my radio
and the kitchen walls
are yellow.
I keep dumping bottles
and listening
for footsteps.

I hope that death contains
less than this.

there are many single women in the world
with one or two or three children
and one wonders where the husbands
have gone or where the lovers have
gone
leaving behind
all those hands and eyes and feet
and voices.
as I pass through their homes
I like opening cupboards and
looking in
or under the sink
or in a closet—
I expect to find the husband
or lover and he'll tell me:
"hey, buddy, didn't you notice her
stretch-marks, she's got stretch-marks
and floppy tits and she eats
onions all the time and farts . . . but
I'm a handy man. I can fix things,
I know how to use a turret-lathe and
I make my own oil changes. I can shoot
pool, bowl, and I can finish 5th or
6th in any cross-country marathon
anywhere. I've got a set of golf
clubs, can shoot in the 80's. I know
where the clit is and what to do about
it. I've got a cowboy hat with the brim
turned straight up at the sides.
I'm good with the lasso and the dukes
and I know all the latest dance steps."

and I'll say, "look, I was just leaving."
and I *will* leave before he can challenge me
to arm-wrestling

or tell a dirty joke
or show me the dancing tattoo on his
right bicep.

but really
all I find in the cupboards are
coffee cups and large cracked brown plates
and under the sink a stack of hardened
rags, and in the closet—more coathangers
than clothes, and it's not until she shows
me the photo album and the photos of him—
nice enough like a shoehorn, or a cart in
the supermarket whose wheels aren't stuck—
that the self-doubt leaves, and the
pages turn and there's one child on a
swing wearing a red outfit and there's
the other one
chasing a seagull in Santa Monica.
and life becomes sad and not dangerous
and therefore good enough:
to have her bring you a cup of coffee in
one of those coffee cups without *him*
jumping out.

stolen

I keep thinking it will be outside
now
waiting for me
blue
front bumper twisted
Maltese cross hanging
from the mirror.
rubber floormat
twisted under the pedals.
20 m.p.g.
good old TRV 491
the faithful love of a man,
the way I put her into second
while taking a corner
the way she could dig from a signal
with any other around.
the way we conquered large and
small spaces
rain
sun
smog
hostility
the crush of things.

I came out of last Thursday night's
fights at the Olympic
and my 1967 Volks was gone
with another lover
to another place.

the fights had been good.
I called a cab at a Standard station
and sat eating a jelly doughnut
with coffee in a cafe and
waited,

and I knew that if I found
the man who stole her
I would kill him.

the cab came. I waved to the
driver, paid for the coffee and
doughnut, got out into the night,
got in, and told him, "Hollywood
and Western," and that particular
night was just about over.

the meek have inherited

if I suffer at this
typewriter
think how I'd feel
among the lettuce-
pickers of Salinas?

I think of the men
I've known in
factories
with no way to
get out—
choking while living
choking while laughing
at Bob Hope or Lucille
Ball while
2 or 3 children beat
tennis balls against
the walls.

some suicides are never
recorded.

the insane always loved
me

and the subnormal.
all through grammar school
junior high
high school
junior college
the unwanted would attach
themselves to
me.
guys with one arm
guys with twitches
guys with speech defects
guys with white film
over one eye,
cowards
misanthropes
killers
peep-freaks
and thieves.
and all through the
factories and on the
bum
I always drew the
unwanted. they found me
right off and attached
themselves. they
still do.
in this neighborhood now
there's one who's
found me.
he pushes around a
shopping cart
filled with trash:
broken canes, shoelaces,
empty potato chip bags,

milk cartons, newspapers, penholders . . .
"hey, buddy, how ya doin'?"
I stop and we talk a
while.
then I say goodbye
but he still follows
me
past the beer
parlours and the
love parlours . . .
"keep me *informed,*
buddy, keep me *informed,*
I want to know what's
going on."
he's my new one.
I've never seen him
talk to anybody
else.
the cart rattles
along a little bit
behind me
then something
falls out.
he stops to pick
it up.
as he does I
walk through the
front door of the
green hotel on the
corner
pass down through
the hall
come out the back
door and
there's a cat
shitting there in
absolute delight,
he grins at
me.

Big Max

in junior high school
Big Max was a problem.
we'd be sitting during lunch hour
eating our peanut butter sandwiches
and potato chips.
he was hairy of nostril
and of eyebrow, his lips
glistened with spittle.
he already wore size ten and a half
shoes. his shirts stretched across a
massive chest. his wrists looked like
two by fours. and he walked up
through the shadows behind the gym
where we sat, my friend Eli and I.
"you guys," he stood there, "you guys
sit with your shoulders slumped!
you walk around with your shoulders
slumped! how are you ever going to
make it?"

we didn't answer.

then Max would look at me.
"stand up!"

I'd stand up and he'd walk around
behind me and say, "square your
shoulders like this!"

and he'd snap my shoulders back.
"there! doesn't that feel *better?*"

"yeah, Max."

then he'd walk off and I'd resume a
normal posture.

Big Max was ready for the
world. it made us sick
to look at him.

trapped

in the winter walking on my
ceiling my eyes the size of street-
lamps. I have 4 feet like a mouse but
wash my own underwear—bearded and
hungover and a hard-on and no lawyer. I
have a face like a washrag. I sing
love songs and carry steel.

I would rather die than cry. I can't
stand hounds can't live without them.
I hang my head against the white
refrigerator and want to scream like
the last weeping of life forever but
I am bigger than the mountains.

call it love
stand it up in the failing
light
put it in a dress
pray sing beg cry laugh
turn off the lights
turn on the radio
add trimmings:
butter, raw eggs, yesterday's
newspaper;
one new shoelace, then add
paprika, sugar, salt, pepper,
phone your drunken aunt in
Calexico;
call it love, you
skewer it good, add
cabbage and applesauce,
then heat it from the
left side,
then heat it from the right
side,
put it in a box
give it away
leave it on a doorstep
vomiting as you go
into the
hydrangea.

on the continent

I'm soft. I
dream too.
I let myself dream. I dream of
being famous. I dream of
walking the streets of London and
Paris. I dream of
sitting in cafes
drinking fine wines and
taking a taxi back to a good
hotel.
I dream of
meeting beautiful ladies in the hall
and
turning them away because
I have a sonnet in mind that
I want to write
before sunrise. at sunrise
I will be asleep and there will be a
strange cat curled up on the
windowsill.

I think we all feel like this
now and then.
I'd even like to visit
Andernach, Germany, the place where
I began. then I'd like to
fly on to Moscow to check out
their mass transit system so
I'd have something faintly lewd to
whisper into the ear of the mayor of
Los Angeles upon my return to this
fucking place.

it could happen.
I'm ready.

I've watched snails climb over
ten foot walls and
vanish.

you mustn't confuse this with
ambition.
I would be able to laugh at my
good turn of the cards—

and I won't forget you.
I'll send postcards and
snapshots, and the
finished sonnet.

12:18 a.m.

beheaded in the middle of the
night
scratching my sides
I am covered with bites
kick my white legs out of the sheets
as the sirens scream
there is a gun blast.

I go to the kitchen
for a glass of water
destroy the reverie of a roach
destroy the roach.
a gale comes from the North
as the man in the apartment across
from me
inserts his penis into the rump of his
4 year old
daughter.

I hear the screams
light a cigar
stick it into the lips of my
beheaded head.
it is half a cigar
stale
a *Medalist Naturáles*, No. 7.

I walk back to the bedroom
with a spray can.
I press the button.
it hisses. I
gag,
think of ancient wars
loves dead.

so much happens in the dark
yet tomorrow
the sun will move up and on,
you'll get a ticket if you park on the
south side of the street on
Thursday
or the north side on
Friday.

the efficiency of the sun and the
law
bulwarks sanity.

something bites me.
I madden
spray half my
bedsheets.

I turn
see the dark mirror—
the cigar
the loose belly
me
old.

I laugh.

it's good they don't
know.

I take my head

put it back on my
neck

get between the sheets and

can't sleep.

yellow cab

the Mexican dancer shook her fans at
me and her ass at me, I
didn't ask her to and
my woman got mad and ran out of the cafe and
it began raining and you could hear it on the
roof and I didn't have a job and I had 13 days left
on the rent.
sometimes when a woman runs out on you like
that you wonder if it's not
economics, you can't blame them—
if I had to get fucked I'd rather get fucked
by somebody with money.
we're all scared but when you're ugly and you
don't have much left you get
strong, and I called the waiter over and I said,
I think I am going to turn this table over, I'm
bored, I'm insane, I need
action, call in your goon, I'll piss on his
collarbone.

I got
thrown out swiftly. it was
raining. I picked myself up in the rain and
walked down the empty street
cotton candy sweet
dumb shit for sale, all the little stores locked
with 67¢ Woolworth locks.

I reached the end of the street in time
to see her get into the yellow cab with
another guy.

I fell down by a garbage can, stood up
and pissed against it, feeling sad and not
sad, knowing there was only so much they could do to

you, piss sliding down the corrugated
tin, the philosophers must have had something to
say about this. women. their luck against your
destiny. winner take Barcelona. next
bar.

how come you're not unlisted?

the men phone and ask me that.

are you really Charles Bukowski
the writer? they ask.

I'm a sometimes writer, I say,
most often I don't do anything.

listen, they ask, I like your
stuff—do you mind if I come
over and bring a couple of 6
packs?

you can bring them, I say
if *you* don't come in . . .

when the women phone, I say,
o yes, I *write*, I'm a writer
only I'm not writing right now.

I feel foolish phoning you,
they say, and I was surprised
to find you listed in the phone book.

I have reasons, I say,
by the way why don't you come over
for a beer?

you wouldn't mind?

and they arrive
handsome women
good of mind and body and eye.

often there isn't sex
but I'm used to that
yet it's good
very good just to look at them—
and some rare times
I have unexpected good luck
otherwise.

for a man of 55 who didn't get laid
until he was 23
and not very often until he was 50
I think that I should stay listed
via Pacific Telephone
until I get as much as
the average man has had.

of course, I'll have to keep
writing immortal poems
but the inspiration is there.

weather report

I suppose it's raining in some Spanish town
now
while I'm feeling bad
like this;
I'd like to think so
now.
let's go to a Mexican hamlet—
that sounds nice:
a Mexican hamlet
while I'm feeling bad
like this
the walls yellow with age—
that rain
out there,
a pig moving in his pen at night
disturbed by the rain,
little eyes like cigarette-ends,
and his damned tail:
see it?
I can't imagine the people.
it's hard for me to imagine the people.
maybe they are feeling bad like this,
almost as bad as this.
I wonder what they do when they feel
bad?
they probably don't mention it.
they say,
"look, it's raining."
that's the best way.

clean old man

here I'll be
55 in a
week.

what will I
write about
when it no
longer stands
up in the morning?

my critics
will love it
when my playground
narrows down to
tortoises
and shellstars.

they might even
say
nice things about
me

as if I had
finally
come to my
senses.

something

I'm out of matches.
the springs in my couch
are broken.
they stole my footlocker.
they stole my oil painting of
two pink eyes.
my car broke down.
eels climb my bathroom walls.
my love is broken.
but the stockmarket went up
today.

a plate glass window

dogs and angels are not
very different.
I often go to this place
to eat
about 2:30 in the afternoon
because all the people who eat
there are particularly addled
simply glad to be alive and
eating baked beans
near a plate glass window
which holds the heat
and doesn't let the cars and
sidewalks inside.

we are allowed as much free
coffee as we can drink
and we sit and quietly drink
the black strong coffee.

it is good to be sitting someplace
in a world at 2:30 in the afternoon
without having the flesh ripped from
your bones. even
being addled, we know this.

nobody bothers us
we bother nobody.

angels and dogs are not
very different
at 2:30 in the afternoon.

I have my favorite table
and after I have finished
I stack the plates, saucers,

the cup, the silverware
neatly—
my offering to the luck—
and that sun
working good
all up and
down
inside the
darkness
here.

junkies

"she shoots up in the neck," she told
me. I told her to stick it into my
ass and she tried and said, "oh oh,"
and I said, "what the hell's the matter?"
she said, "nothing, this is New York
style," and she jammed it in again and said,
"oh shit." I took it and put it into
my arm, I got part of it.
"I don't know why people
fuck with the stuff, there's not that
much to it. I think they're all losers
and they want to lose real bad. there's
no other way, it's like they can't
get where they're going or want to go
and there's no other way.
this has got to be it.
she shoots up in the neck."

"I know," I said. "I phoned her, she
could hardly talk, said it was
laryngitis. have some of this wine."

it was white wine and 4:30 a.m. and her
daughter was sleeping in the bedroom. she
had cable tv with no sound and
a large screen young John Wayne watched
us, and we neither kissed nor made
love and I left at 6:15 a.m.
after the beer and wine were gone
so her daughter wouldn't awaken for
school and find me sitting in
bed with her mother
with John Wayne and the night gone
and not much chance for anybody—

99 to one

the blazing shark
wants my balls
as I walk through the meat section
looking for salami and cheese

purple housewives
fingering 75 cent avocados
know my shopping cart is an
oversized cock

I am a man with a switchball watch
standing in a honky-tonk phonebooth
sucking strawberry red titty
upsidedown in a Philadelphia crowd.

suddenly all about me are screams of
RAPE RAPE RAPE RAPE RAPE
and I am stiffing it to something beneath me
dyed red hair, bad breath, blue teeth

I used to like Monet
I used to like Monet very much
it was funny, I thought, the way he did it
with colors

women are so expensive
dog leashes are expensive
I am going to start selling air in dark orange bags
marked: moon-blooms

I used to like bottles full of blood
young girls in camel-hair coats
Prince Valiant
Popeye's magic touch

the struggle is in the struggle
like a corkscrew
a good man doesn't get cork in the wine

the thought has occurred to millions of men
while shaving
the removal of life might be preferred to
the removal of hair

spit out cotton and clean your rearview
mirror, run like you mean it, drunk jock,
the whores will win, the fools will win,
but break like a horse out of the gate.

the crunch

too much
too little

too fat
too thin
or nobody.

laughter or
tears

haters
lovers

strangers with faces like
the backs of
thumb tacks

armies running through
streets of blood
waving winebottles
bayoneting and fucking
virgins.

or an old guy in a cheap room
with a photograph of M. Monroe.

there is a loneliness in this world so great
that you can see it in the slow movement of
the hands of a clock.

people so tired
mutilated
either by love or no love.

people just are not good to each other
one on one.

the rich are not good to the rich
the poor are not good to the poor.

we are afraid.

our educational system tells us
that we can all be
big-ass winners.

it hasn't told us
about the gutters
or the suicides.

or the terror of one person
aching in one place
alone

untouched
unspoken to

watering a plant.

people are not good to each other.
people are not good to each other.
people are not good to each other.

I suppose they never will be.
I don't ask them to be.

but sometimes I think about
it.

the beads will swing
the clouds will cloud
and the killer will behead the child
like taking a bite out of an ice cream cone.

too much
too little

too fat
too thin
or nobody

more haters than lovers.

people are not good to each other.
perhaps if they were
our deaths would not be so sad.

meanwhile I look at young girls
stems
flowers of chance.

there must be a way.

surely there must be a way we have not yet
thought of.

who put this brain inside of me?

it cries
it demands
it says that there is a chance.

it will not say
"no."

a horse with greenblue eyes

what you see is what you see:
madhouses are rarely
on display.

that we still walk about and
scratch ourselves and light
cigarettes

is more the miracle

than bathing beauties
than roses and the moth.

to sit in a small room
and drink a can of beer
and roll a cigarette
while listening to Brahms
on a small red radio

is to have come back
from a dozen wars
alive

listening to the sound
of the refrigerator

as bathing beauties rot

and the oranges and apples
roll away.

3

Scarlet

Scarlet

I'm glad when they arrive
and I'm glad when they leave

I'm glad when I hear their heels
approaching my door
and I'm glad when those heels
walk away

I'm glad to fuck
I'm glad to care
and I'm glad when it's over

and
since it's always either
starting or finishing
I'm glad
most of the time

and the cats walk up and down
and the earth spins around the sun
and the phone rings:

"this is Scarlet."

"who?"

"Scarlet."

"o.k., get it on over."

and I hang up thinking
maybe this is it

go in
take a quick shit
shave

bathe

dress

dump the sacks
and cartons of empty
bottles

sit down to the sound of
heels approaching
more an army approaching than
victory

it's Scarlet
and in my kitchen the faucet
keeps dripping
needs a washer.

I'll take care of it
later.

red up and down

red hair
real
she whirled it
and she asked
"is my ass still on?"

such comedy.

there is always one woman
to save you from another

and as that woman saves you
she makes ready to
destroy.

"sometimes I hate you,"
she said.

she walked out and sat on
my porch and read my copy
of Catullus, she stayed out
there for an hour.

people walked up and down
past my place
wondering where such an ugly
old man could get
such beauty.

I didn't know either.

when she walked in I grabbed
her and pulled her to my lap.
I lifted my glass and told
her, "drink this."

"oh," she said, "you've mixed
wine with Jim Beam, you're gonna
get nasty."

"you henna your hair, don't
you?"

"you don't *look*," she said and
stood up and pulled down her
slacks and panties and
the hair down there was the
same as the hair
up there.

Catullus himself couldn't have wished
for more historic or
wondrous grace;
then he went
goofy

for tender boys
not mad enough
to become
women.

like a flower in the rain

I cut the middle fingernail of the middle
finger
right hand
real short
and I began rubbing along her cunt
as she sat upright in bed
spreading lotion over her arms
face
and breasts
after bathing.
then she lit a cigarette:
"don't let this put you off,"
and smoked and continued to rub the
lotion on.
I continued to rub the cunt.
"you want an apple?" I asked.
"sure," she said, "you got one?"
but I got to her—
she began to twist
then she rolled on her side,
she was getting wet and open
like a flower in the rain.
then she rolled on her stomach
and her most beautiful ass
looked up at me
and I reached under and got the
cunt again.
she reached around and got my
cock, she rolled and twisted,
I mounted
my face falling into the mass
of red hair that overflowed
from her head
and my fattened cock entered
into the miracle.

later we joked about the lotion
and the cigarette and the apple.
then I went out and got some chicken
and shrimp and french fries and buns
and mashed potatoes and gravy and
cole slaw, and we ate. she told me
how good she felt and I told her
how good I felt and we ate
the chicken and the shrimp and the
french fries and the buns and the
mashed potatoes and the gravy and
the cole slaw too.

light brown

light brown stare

that dumb blank marvelous
light brown stare

I'll take care of
it.

you needn't carry me
anymore
with your Cleopatra
movie star
tricks

do you realize
that if I were an adding machine
I might break down
tabulating
how many times you've used
that light brown stare?

not that you're not the best
with your light brown stare.

someday some crazy son of a bitch
is going to murder you

and you'll cry out my name
you'll finally know
what you should have known

so very long
ago.

huge ear rings

I go to pick her up.
she's on some errand.
she always has errands
many things to do.
I have nothing to do.

she comes out of her apartment
I see her move toward my car

she is barefooted
dressed casually
except for huge ear rings.

I light a cigarette
and when I look up
she is stretched out on the street

a quite busy street

all 112 pounds of her
as beautiful as anything you might
imagine.

I switch on the radio
and wait for her to get up.

she does.

I flip the car door open.
she gets in. I drive away from the
curb. she likes the song on the radio
she turns the radio up.

she seems to like all the songs
she seems to know all the songs

each time I see her she looks better
and better

200 years ago they would have burned her
at the stake

now she puts on her
mascara as we
drive along.

she came out of the bathroom with
her flaming red hair and said—

the cops want me to come down and identify
some guy who tried to rape me.
I've lost the key to my car again; I've got
the key to open the door but not the one
to start it.
those people are trying to take my child
away from me but I won't let them.
Rochelle almost o.d.'d, then she went at
Harry with something, and he punched her.
she's had those cracked ribs, you know,
and one of them punctured her lung. she's
down at the county under a machine.

where's my comb?
your comb has all that guck in it.

I told her,
I haven't seen your
comb.

a killer

consistency is terrific:
shark-mouth
grubby interior with an
almost perfect body,
long blazing hair—
it confuses me
and others

she runs from man to man
offering endearments

she speaks of love

then breaks each man
to her will

shark-mouthed
grubby interior

we see it too late:
after the cock gets swallowed
the heart follows

her long blazing hair
her almost perfect body
walks down the street
as the same sun
falls upon flowers.

longshot

she's not for you, man,
she's not your type,
she's erased
she's been used
she's got all the wrong
habits,
he told me
in between races.

I'm going to bet the 4
horse, I told him.
well, it's only that I'd
like to turn her around
in mid-stream,
save her, you might say.

you can't save her, he said,
you're 55, you need kindness.
I'm going to bet the 6 horse.
you're not the one to save
her.

who can save her? I asked.
I don't think the 6 has a
chance, I like the 4.

she needs somebody to beat her
from wall to wall, he said,
kick her ass, she'd love
it. she'd stay home and
wash the dishes.
the 6 horse will be in
the running.

I'm no good at beating women,
I said.

forget her then, he said.

it's hard to, I said.

he got up and bet the 6
and I got up and bet the 4.
the 5 horse won
by 3 lengths
at 15 to one.

she's got red hair
like lightning from heaven,
I said.

forget her, he said.

we tore up our tickets
and stared at the lake
in the center of the track.

it was going to be
a long afternoon
for both of us.

the promise

she bent over the side of the bed
and opened the portfolio
along the side of the wall.
we were drinking.
she said, "you promised me these
paintings once, don't you
remember?"
"what? no, no, I don't remember."
"well, you did," she said, "and you
ought to keep your promises."
"leave those fucking paintings alone,"
I said.
then I walked into the kitchen for
a beer. I paused to vomit
and when I came out
I saw her through my window
going down the court walk
toward her place in back.
she was trying to hurry
and balanced on top of her head
were 40 paintings:
oils
black and whites
acrylics
water colors.
she stumbled once and almost
fell on her ass.
then she ran up her steps
and was gone through her door
to her place upstairs
running with all those paintings
on top of her head.
it was one of the funniest damned
things I ever did see.

well, I guess I'll just have to
paint 40 more.

waving and waving goodbye

I paid this one's fare all the way from Houston
to San Francisco
then flew up to meet her at her brother's house
and I got drunk
and talked all night about a redhead, and
she finally said, "you sleep up there,"
and I climbed the ladder
up into a bunk and she slept
down there.

the next day they drove me to the airport
and I flew back, thinking, well,
there's still the redhead and when I got back in
I phoned the redhead and said, "I'm back, baby,
I flew up to see this woman and I talked about
you all night, so here I am . . ."

"well, why don't you fly back up and finish
the job?" she said and hung up.

then I got drunk and the phone rang
and they said they were
two ladies from Germany and they'd like
to see me.

so they came over and one was 20 and the
other was 22. I told them that my heart
had been smashed for the last time and
that I was giving up women. they laughed
at me and we drank and smoked and went to
bed together.

I got this thing in front of me and
first I grabbed one and then I grabbed the
other.

I finally settled on the 22 year old and
ate her up.

they stayed 2 days and 2 nights
but I never got to the 20 year old,
she was on tampax.

I finally drove them to Sherman Oaks
and they stood at the foot of a long
driveway
waving and waving goodbye as I backed
my Volks out.

when I got back there was a letter from a
lady in Eureka. she said that she wanted me
to fuck her until she couldn't
walk anymore.

I stretched out and whacked-off
thinking about a little girl I had seen
on a red bicycle about a week ago.

then I took a bath and put on my green
terrycloth robe just in time to get the fights
on tv from the Olympic.

there was a black and a Chicano in there.
that always made a good fight.

and it was a good idea too:
put them in there and let them kill each
other.

I watched the whole fight
thinking about the redhead all the time.

I think the Chicano won
but I'm not sure.

liberty

she was sitting in the window
of room 1010 at the Chelsea
in New York,
Janis Joplin's old room.
it was 104 degrees
and she was on speed
and had one leg over
the sill,
and she leaned out and said,
"God, this is great!"
and then she slipped
and almost went out,
just catching herself.
it was very close.
she pulled herself in
walked over and stretched
on the bed.

I've lost a lot of women
in a lot of different ways
but that would have been
the first time
that way.

then she rolled off the bed
landed on her back
and when I walked over
she was asleep.

all day she had been wanting
to see the Statue of Liberty.
now she wouldn't worry me about that
for a while.

don't touch the girls

she's up seeing my doctor
trying to get some diet pills;
she's not fat, she needs the speed.
I go down to the nearest bar and wait.
at 3:30 in the afternoon of a tuesday.
they have a dancer.

there's only one other man in the bar.

she works out
looking at herself in the mirror.
she's like a monkey
dark
Korean.

she's not very good,
skinny and obvious
and she sticks her tongue out at me
then at the other man.

times must be truly hard, I think.

I have a few more beers then get up to leave.
she waves me over.
"you go?" she asks.
"yes," I say, "my wife has cancer."

I shake her hand.

she points to a sign behind her:
DON'T TOUCH THE GIRLS.

she points to the sign and says,
"the sign says, 'DON'T TOUCH THE GIRLS'."

I go back to the parking lot and wait.
she comes out.
"did you get the pills?" I ask.
"yes," she says.
"then it's been a successful day."

I think of the dancer walking across my
kitchen. I can't visualize it. I am going
to die alone
just the way I live.

"take me to my place," she says,
"I've got to get ready for night school."

"sure," I say and drive her on in.

dark shades

I never wear dark shades
but this red head went to get
a prescription filled on Hollywood Blvd.
and she kept haggling and working at
me, snapping and snarling.
I left her at the prescription counter
and walked around and got a large tube of
Crest and a giant bottle of Joy.
then I walked up to
the dark shade display rack and bought
the most vicious pair of shades
I could find.
we paid for our things
walked down to a Mexican place
and she ordered a taco she couldn't eat
and sat there
haggling and snapping and snarling at me
and after eating I ordered 3 beers
drank them down
then put on my shades.
"o my God," she said, "o my God shit!"
and I ripped her up both sides
most excellent riposte
snarling stinking marmalade shots
shit blows
farts from hell,
then I got up
paid
she following me out
both of us in shades
and the sidewalks split.
we found her car
got in and drove off
me sitting there
pushing the shades back against my nose

ripping out her backbone
and waving it out the window
like a broken Confederate flagpole . . .
dark and vicious shades help.
"o my God shit!" she said,
and the sun was up
and I didn't know it.

they were a bargain for $4.25
even though I had left the Crest
and the Joy behind
at the taco place.

prayer in bad weather

by God, I don't know what to
do.
they're so nice to have around.
they have a way of playing with
the balls
and looking at the cock very
seriously
turning it
tweeking it
examining each part
as their long hair falls on
your belly.

it's not the fucking and sucking
alone that reaches into a man
and softens him, it's the extras,
it's all the extras.

now it's raining tonight
and there's nobody
they are elsewhere
examining things
in new bedrooms
in new moods
or maybe in old
bedrooms.

anyhow, it's raining tonight,
one hell of a dashing, pouring
rain. . . .

very little to do.
I've read the newspaper
paid the gas bill
the electric co.
the phone bill.

it keeps raining.

they soften a man
and then let him swim
in his own juice.

I need an old-fashioned whore
at the door tonight
closing her green umbrella,
drops of moonlit rain on her
purse, saying, "shit, man,
can't you get better music
than *that* on your radio?
and turn up the heat . . ."

it's always when a man's swollen
with love and everything
else
that it keeps raining
splattering
flooding
rain
good for the trees and the
grass and the air . . .
good for things that
live alone.

I would give anything
for a female's hand on me
tonight.
they soften a man and
then leave him
listening to the rain.

melancholia

the history of melancholia
includes all of us.

me, I writhe in dirty sheets
while staring at blue walls
and nothing.

I have gotten so used to melancholia
that
I greet it like an old
friend.

I will now do 15 minutes of grieving
for the lost redhead,
I tell the gods.

I do it and feel quite bad
quite sad,
then I rise
CLEANSED
even though nothing is
solved.

that's what I get for kicking
religion in the ass.

I should have kicked the redhead
in the ass
where her brains and her bread and
butter are
at . . .

but, no, I've felt sad
about everything:

the lost redhead was just another
smash in a lifelong
loss . . .

I listen to drums on the radio now
and grin.

there is something wrong with me
besides
melancholia.

a stethoscope case

my doctor has just come into his office
from surgery.
he meets me in the men's john.
"God damn," he says to me,
"where did you find her? oh, I just like
to *look* at girls like that!"
I tell him: "it's my specialty: cement
hearts and beautiful bodies. If you can find
a heart-beat, let me know."
"I'll take good care of her," he says.
"yes, and please remember all the ethical
codes of your honorable profession," I tell
him.

he zips up first then washes.
"how's your health?" he asks.

"physically I'm sound as a tic. mentally I'm
wasted, doomed, on my tiny cross, all that
crap."

"I'll take good care of her."

"yes. and let me know about the heart-beat."

he walks out.
I finish, zip up and also walk out.
only I don't wash up.

I'm far beyond all that.

eat your heart out

I've come by, she says, to tell you
that this is it. I'm not kidding, it's
over. this is it.

I sit on the couch watching her arrange
her long red hair before my bedroom
mirror.
she pulls her hair up and
piles it on top of her head—
she lets her eyes look at
my eyes—
then she drops the hair and
lets it fall down in front of her face.

we go to bed and I hold her
speechlessly from the back
my arm around her neck
I touch her wrists and hands
feel up to
her elbows
no further.

she gets up.

this is it, she says,
eat your heart out. you
got any rubber bands?

I don't know.

here's one, she says,
this will do. well,
I'm going.

I get up and walk her
to the door

just as she leaves
she says,
I want you to buy me
some high-heeled shoes
with tall thin spikes,
black high-heeled shoes.
no, I want them
red.

I watch her walk down the cement walk
under the trees
she walks all right and
as the poinsettas drip in the sun
I close the door.

the retreat

this time has finished me.

I feel like the German troops
whipped by snow and the communists
walking bent
with newspapers stuffed into
worn boots.

my plight is just as terrible.
maybe more so.

victory was so close
victory was there.

as she stood before my mirror
younger and more beautiful than
any woman I had ever known
combing yards and yards of red hair
as I watched her.

and when she came to bed
she was more beautiful than ever
and the love was very very good.

eleven months.

now she's gone
gone as they go.

this time has finished me.

it's a long road back

and back to where?

the guy ahead of me
falls.

I step over him.

did she get him too?

I made a mistake

I reached up into the top of the closet
and took out a pair of blue panties
and showed them to her and
asked "are these yours?"

and she looked and said,
"no, those belong to a dog."

she left after that and I haven't seen
her since. she's not at her place.
I keep going there, leaving notes stuck
into the door. I go back and the notes
are still there. I take the Maltese cross
cut it down from my car mirror, tie it
to her doorknob with a shoelace, leave
a book of poems.
when I go back the next night everything
is still there.

I keep searching the streets for that
blood-wine battleship she drives
with a weak battery, and the doors
hanging from broken hinges.

I drive around the streets
an inch away from weeping,
ashamed of my sentimentality and
possible love.

a confused old man driving in the rain
wondering where the good luck
went.

4

popular melodies
in the last of
your mind

girls in pantyhose

schoolgirls in pantyhose
sitting on bus stop benches
looking tired at 13
with their raspberry lipstick.
it's hot in the sun
and the day at school has been
dull, and going home is
dull, and
I drive by in my car
peering at their warm legs.
their eyes look
away—
they've been warned
about ruthless and horny old
studs; they're just not going
to give it away like that.
and yet it's dull
waiting out the minutes on
the bench and the years at
home, and the books they
carry are dull and the food
they eat is dull, and even
the ruthless, horny old studs
are dull.

the girls in pantyhose wait,
they await the proper time and
moment, and then they will move
and then they will conquer.

I drive around in my car
peeking up their legs
pleased that I will never be
part of their heaven and
their hell. but that scarlet

lipstick on those sad waiting
mouths! it would be nice to
kiss each of them once, fully,
then give them back.
but the bus will
get them first.

up your yellow river

a woman told a man
when he got off a plane
that I was dead.
a magazine printed
the fact that I was dead
and somebody else said
that they'd heard that I
was dead, and then somebody
wrote an article and said
our Rimbaud our Villon is
dead. at the same time an old
drinking buddy published
a piece stating that I
could no longer write. a
real Judas job. they can't
wait for me to go, these
farts. well, I'm listening
to Tchaikovsky's piano
concerto number one and
the announcer said Mahler's
5th and 10th symphonies
are coming up via
Amsterdam,
and the beerbottles are
on the floor and ash
from my cigarettes
covers my cotton under-
wear and my gut, I've
told all my girlfriends to
go to hell, and even this
is a better poem than any
of those gravediggers
could write.

artists:

she wrote me for years.
"I'm drinking wine in the kitchen.
it's raining outside. the children
are in school."

she was an average citizen
worried about her soul, her typewriter
and her
underground poetry reputation.

she wrote fairly well and with honesty
but only long after others had
broken the road ahead.

she'd phone me drunk at 2 a.m.
at 3 a.m.
while her husband slept.

"it's good to hear your voice," she'd
say.

"it's good to hear your voice too," I'd
say.

what the hell, you
know.

she finally came down. I think it had
something to do with
The Chapparal Poets Society of California.
they had to elect officers. she phoned me
from their hotel.

"I'm here," she said, "we're going to elect
officers."

"o.k., fine," I said, "get some good ones."

I hung up.

the phone rang again.
"hey, don't you want to see me?"

"sure," I said, "what's the address?"

after she said goodbye I jacked-off
changed my stockings
drank a half bottle of wine and
drove on out.

they were all drunk and trying to
fuck each other.

I drove her back to my place.

she had on pink panties with
ribbons.

we drank some beer and
smoked and talked about
Ezra Pound, then we
slept.

it's no longer clear to
me whether I drove her to
the airport or
not.

she still writes letters
and I answer each one
viciously
hoping to make her
stop.

someday she may luck into
fame like Erica

Jong. (her face is not as good
but her body is better)
and I'll think,
my God, what have I done?
I blew it.
or rather: I didn't blow
it.

meanwhile I have her box number
and I'd better inform her
that my second novel will be out
in September.
that ought to keep her nipples hard
while I consider the possibility of
Francine du Plessix Gray.

I have shit stains in
my underwear too

I hear them outside:
"does he always type this
late?"
"no, it's very unusual."
"he shouldn't type this
late."
"he hardly ever does."
"does he drink?"
"I think he does."
"he went to the mailbox in
his underwear yesterday."
"I saw him too."
"he doesn't have any friends."
"he's old."
"he shouldn't type this late."

they go inside and it begins
to rain as
3 gun shots sound half a block
away and
one of the skyscrapers in
downtown L.A. begins
burning
25 foot flames licking toward
doom.

this guy
he's got a crazy eye
and he's brown
a dark brown from the sun
the Hollywood and Western sun
the racetrack sun
he sees me and he says,
"hey, Hawley's leaving town
for a week. he messes up
my handicapping. now
I've got a chance."

he's grinning, he means it:
with Hawley out of town
he's going to move toward
that castle in the Hollywood Hills;
dancing girls
six German Shepherds
a drawbridge,
ten year old
wine.

Sam the Whorehouse Man
walks up and I tell Sam that
I am clearing $150 a day
at the track.
"I work right off the
toteboard," I tell him.
"I need a girl," he tells me,
"who can belt-buckle a guy
without coming out with all
this Christian moral bullshit
afterwards."

"Hawley's leaving town,"
I tell Sam.

"where's the Shoe?"
he asks.
"back east," says an old man
who's standing there.
he has a white plastic shield
over his left eye
with little holes
punched into it.

"that leaves it all to Pinky,"
says dark brown.

we all stand looking at each
other.
then
a silent signal given
we turn away
and start walking,
each
in a different direction:
north south east west.

we know something.

an unkind poem

they go on writing
pumping out poems—
young boys and college professors
wives who drink wine all afternoon
while their husbands work,
they go on writing
the same names in the same magazines
everybody writing a little worse each year,
getting out a poetry collection
and pumping out more poems
it's like a contest
it is a contest
but the prize is invisible.

they won't write short stories or articles
or novels
they just go on
pumping out poems
each sounding more and more like the others
and less and less like themselves,
and some of the young boys weary and quit
but the professors never quit
and the wives who drink wine in the afternoons
never ever ever quit
and new young boys arrive with new magazines
and there is some correspondence with lady or men poets
and some fucking
and everything is exaggerated and dull.

when the poems come back
they retype them
and send them off to the next magazine on the list,
and they give *readings*
all the readings they can
for free most of the time

hoping that somebody will finally know
finally applaud them
finally congratulate and recognize their
talent
they are all so sure of their genius
there is so little self-doubt,
and most of them live in North Beach or New York City,
and their faces are like their poems:
alike,
and they know each other and
gather and hate and admire and choose and discard
and keep pumping out more poems
more poems
more poems
the contest of the dullards:
tap tap tap, tap tap, tap tap tap, tap tap . . .

the bee

I suppose like any other boy
I had one best friend in the neighborhood.
his name was Eugene and he was bigger
than I was and one year older.
Eugene used to whip me pretty good.
we fought all the time.
I kept trying him but without much
success.

once we leaped off a garage roof together
to prove our guts.
I twisted my ankle and he came up clean
as freshly-wrapped butter.

I guess the only good thing he ever did for me
was when the bee stung me while I was barefoot
and while I sat down and pulled the stinger out
he said,
"I'll get the son of a bitch!"

and he did
with a tennis racket
plus a rubber hammer.

it was all right
they say they die
anyway.

my foot swelled up double-size
and I stayed in bed
praying for death

and Eugene went on to become an
Admiral or a Commander
or something large in the United States Navy

and he passed through one or two wars
without injury.

I imagine him an old man now
in a rocking chair
with his false teeth
and glass of buttermilk . . .

while drunk
I fingerfuck this 19 year old groupie
in bed with me.

but the worst part is
(like jumping off the garage roof)
Eugene wins again
because he's not even thinking
about me.

the most

here comes the fishhead singing
here comes the baked potato in drag

here comes nothing to do all day long
here comes another night of no sleep

here comes the phone ringing the wrong tone

here comes a termite with a banjo
here comes a flagpole with blank eyes
here comes a cat and a dog wearing nylons

here comes a machinegun singing
here comes bacon burning in the pan
here comes a voice saying something dull

here comes a newspaper stuffed with small red birds
with flat brown beaks

here comes a cunt carrying a torch
a grenade
a deathly love

here comes victory carrying
one bucket of blood
and stumbling over the berrybush

and the sheets hang out the windows

and the bombers head east west north south
get lost
get tossed like salad

as all the fish in the sea line up and form
one line

one long line
one very long thin line
the longest line you could ever imagine

and we get lost
walking past purple mountains

we walk lost
bare at last like the knife

having given
having spit it out like an unexpected olive seed

as the girl at the call service
screams over the phone:
"don't call back! you sound like a jerk!"

ah . . .

drinking German beer
and trying to come up with
the immortal poem at
5 p.m. in the afternoon.
but, ah, I've told the
students that the thing
to do is not to try.

but when the women aren't
around and the horses aren't
running
what else is there to do?

I've had a couple of
sexual fantasies
had lunch out
mailed three letters
been to the grocery store.
nothing on tv.
the telephone is quiet.
I've run dental floss
between my teeth.

it won't rain and I listen
to the early arrivals from the
8 hour day as they
drive in and park their cars
behind the apartment
next door.

I sit drinking German beer
and trying to come up with the
big one
and I'm not going to make it.
I'm just going to keep drinking

more and more German beer
and rolling smokes
and by 11 p.m.
I'll be spread out
on the unmade bed
face up
asleep under the electric
light
still waiting on the immortal
poem.

the girl on the bus stop bench

I saw her when I was in the left lane
going east on Sunset.
she was sitting
with her legs crossed
reading a paperback.
she was Italian or Indian or
Greek
and I was stopped at a red signal
as now and then a wind
would lift her skirt,
I was directly across from her
looking in,
and such perfect immaculate legs
I had never seen.
I am essentially bashful
but I stared and kept staring
until the person in the car behind
me honked.

it had never happened quite like that
before.
I drove around the block
and parked in the supermarket
lot
directly across from her
in my dark shades
I kept staring
like a schoolboy in his first
excitement.

I memorized her shoes
her dress
her stockings
her face.

cars came by and blocked my
view.
then I saw her again.
the wind flipped her skirt
high along her thighs
and I began rubbing myself.
just before her bus came
I climaxed.
I smelled my sperm
felt it wet against my shorts
and pants.

it was an ugly white bus
and it took her away.

I backed out of the parking lot
thinking, I'm a peep-freak
but at least I didn't expose
myself.

I'm a peep-freak
but why do they do that?
why do they look like that?
why do they let the wind do
that?

when I got home
I undressed and bathed
got out
toweled
turned on
the news
turned off the news
and
wrote this poem.

I'm getting back to where I
was

I used to take the back off
the telephone and stuff it with rags
and when somebody knocked
I wouldn't answer and if they persisted
I'd tell them in terms vulgar
to vanish.

just another old crank
with wings of gold
flabby white belly
plus
eyes to knock out
the sun.

a lovely couple

I had to take a shit
but instead I went
into this shop to
have a key made.
the woman was dressed
in gingham and smelled
like a muskrat.
"Ralph," she hollered
and an old swine in a
flowered shirt and
size 6 shoes, her
husband, came out and
she said, "this man
wants a key."
he started grinding
as if he really didn't
want to.
there were slinking
shadows and urine
in the air.
I moved along the
glass counter,
pointed and called
to her,
"here, I want this
one."
she handed it to
me: a switchblade
in a light purple
case.
$6.50 plus tax.
the key cost
practically
nothing.
I got my change and

walked out on
the street.
sometimes you need
people like that.

the strangest sight you ever did
see—

I had this room in front on DeLongpre
and I used to sit for hours
in the daytime
looking out the front
window.
there were any number of girls who would
walk by
swaying;
it helped my afternoons,
added something to the beer and the
cigarettes.

one day I saw something
extra.
I heard the sound of it first.
"come on, push!" he said.
there was a long board
about 2½ feet wide and
8 feet long;
nailed to the ends and in the middle
were roller skates.
he was pulling in front
two long ropes attached to the board
and she was in back
guiding and also pushing.
all their possessions were tied to the
board:
pots, pans, bedquilts, and so forth
were roped to the board
tied down;
and the skatewheels were grinding.

he was white, red-necked, a
southerner—

thin, slumped, his pants about to
fall from his
ass—
his face pinked by the sun and
cheap wine,
and she was black
and walked upright
pushing;
she was simply beautiful
in turban
long green ear rings
yellow dress
from
neck to
ankle.
her face was gloriously
indifferent.

"don't worry!" he shouted, looking back
at her, "somebody will
rent us a place!"

she didn't answer.

then they were gone
although I still heard the
skatewheels.

they're going to make it,
I thought.

I'm sure they
did.

in a neighborhood of
murder

the roaches spit out
paperclips
and the helicopter circles and circles
smelling for blood
searchlights leering down into our
bedroom

5 guys in this court have pistols
another a
machete
we are all murderers and
alcoholics
but there are worse in the hotel
across the street
they sit in the green and white doorway
banal and depraved
waiting to be institutionalized

here we each have a small green plant
in the window
and when we fight with our women at 3 a.m.
we speak
softly
and on each porch
is a small dish of food
always eaten by morning
we presume
by the
cats.

private first class

they took my man off the street
the other day
he wore an L.A. Rams sweatshirt with
the sleeves cut
off
and under that
an army shirt
private first class
and he wore a green beret
walked very straight
he was black in brown walking shorts
hair dyed blonde
he never bothered anybody
he stole a few babies
and ran off cackling
but he always returned the infants
unharmed
he slept in the back of the
Love Parlor
the girls let him.
compassion is found in
strange places.

one day I didn't see him
then another.
I asked around.

my taxes are going to go up
again. the state's got to
house and feed
him. the cops took him
in. no
good.

love is a dog from hell

feet of cheese
coffeepot soul
hands that hate poolsticks
eyes like paperclips
I prefer red wine
I am bored on airliners
I am docile during earthquakes
I am sleepy at funerals
I puke at parades
and am sacrificial at chess
and cunt and caring
I smell urine in churches
I can no longer read
I can no longer sleep

eyes like paperclips
my green eyes
I prefer white wine

my box of rubbers is getting
stale
I take them out
Trojan-Enz
lubricated
for greater sensitivity
I take them out
and put three of them on

the walls of my bedroom are blue

Linda where did you go?
Katherine where did you go?
(and Nina went to England)

I have toenail clippers
and Windex glass cleaner

229

green eyes
blue bedroom
bright machinegun sun

this whole thing is like a seal
caught on oily rocks
and circled by the Long Beach Marching Band
at 3:36 p.m.

there is a ticking behind me
but no clock
I feel something crawling along
the left side of my nose:
memories of airliners

my mother had false teeth
my father had false teeth
and every Saturday of their lives
they took up all the rugs in their house
waxed the hardwood floors
and covered them with rugs again

and Nina is in England
and Irene is on ATD
and I take my green eyes
and lay down in my blue bedroom.

my groupie

I read last Saturday in the
redwoods outside of Santa Cruz
and I was about 3/4's finished
when I heard a long high scream
and a quite attractive
young girl came running toward me
long gown & divine eyes of fire
and she leaped up on the stage
and screamed: "I WANT YOU!
I WANT YOU! TAKE ME! TAKE
ME!"
I told her, "look, get the hell
away from me."
but she kept tearing at my
clothing and throwing herself
at me.
"where were you," I
asked her, "when I was living
on one candy bar a day and
sending short stories to the
Atlantic Monthly?"
she grabbed my balls and almost
twisted them off. her kisses
tasted like shitsoup.
2 women jumped up on the stage
and
carried her off into the
woods.
I could still hear her screams
as I began the next poem.

maybe, I thought, I should have
taken her on the stage in front
of all those eyes.

but one can never be sure
whether it's good poetry or
bad acid.

*now, if you were teaching creative
writing, he asked, what would you
tell them?*

I'd tell them to have an unhappy love
affair, hemorrhoids, bad teeth
and to drink cheap wine,
avoid opera and golf and chess,
to keep switching the head of their
bed from wall to wall
and then I'd tell them to have
another unhappy love affair
and never to use a silk typewriter
ribbon,
avoid family picnics
or being photographed in a rose
garden;
read Hemingway only once,
skip Faulkner
ignore Gogol
stare at photos of Gertrude Stein
and read Sherwood Anderson in bed
while eating Ritz crackers,
realize that people who keep
talking about sexual liberation
are more frightened than you are.
listen to E. Power Biggs work the
organ on your radio while you're
rolling Bull Durham in the dark
in a strange town
with one day left on the rent
after having given up
friends, relatives and jobs.
never consider yourself superior and /
or fair
and never try to be.
have another unhappy love affair.

watch a fly on a summer curtain.
never try to succeed.
don't shoot pool.
be righteously angry when you
find your car has a flat tire.
take vitamins but don't lift weights or jog.

then after all this
reverse the procedure.
have a good love affair.
and the thing
you might learn
is that nobody knows anything—
not the State, nor the mice
the garden hose or the North Star.
and if you ever catch me
teaching a creative writing class
and you read this back to me
I'll give you a straight A
right up the pickle
barrel.

the good life

a house with 7 or 8 people
living in it
getting up the rent.
there's a stereo never used
and a set of bongos
never used
and there are rugs over the
windows
and you smoke
as the living roaches
stumble over buttons on your
shirt and tumble
off.

it's dark and somebody sends
out for food. you eat the food
and sleep. everybody sleeps at
once: on floors, coffeetables,
couches, beds, in bathtubs. there's
even one in the brush outside.

then somebody wakes up and
says, "come on, let's roll
one!"

a few others wake up.
"sure. yea. o.k."

"all right. come on, somebody
roll a couple. let's get it
on!"

"yeah! let's get it on!"

we smoke a few joints and then
we're asleep again

except we reverse positions:
bathtub to couch, coffeetable to
rug, bed to floor, and a new one
falls into the brush
outside, and they haven't yet
found Patty Hearst and Tim doesn't
want to speak to
Allan.

the Greek

the guy in the front court can't
speak English, he's Greek, a
rather stupid-looking and
fairly ugly man.

now my landlord does some painting,
it's not very good.

he showed the Greek one of his paintings.

the Greek went out and purchased
paper, brushes, paints.

the Greek started painting in his front
court. he leaves the paintings outside to
dry.

the Greek had never painted before—
here it comes:
            a blue guitar
            a street
            a horse.

he's good
in his mid-forties he's
good.
he's found a
toy.
he's happy
now.

then I think, I wonder if he will get
very good?
and I wonder if I will have to watch
the rest?

the glory and the women and the women and
the women and the women and
the decay.

I can almost smell the bloodsuckers forming
to the left.

you see,
I have fastened to him already.

my comrades

this one teaches
that one lives with his mother.
and that one is supported by a red-faced alcoholic father
with the brain of a gnat.
this one takes speed and has been supported by
the same woman for 14 years.
that one writes a novel every ten days
but at least pays his own rent.
this one goes from place to place
sleeping on couches, drinking and making his
spiel.
this one prints his own books on a duplicating
machine.
that one lives in an abandoned shower room
in a Hollywood hotel.
this one seems to know how to get grant after grant,
his life is a filling-out of forms.
this one is simply rich and lives in the best
places while knocking on the best doors.
that one had breakfast with William Carlos
Williams.
and this one teaches.
and that one teaches.
and this one puts out textbooks on how to do it
and speaks in a cruel and dominating voice.

they are everywhere.
everybody is a writer.
and almost every writer is a poet.
poets poets poets   poets poets poets
poets poets poets   poets poets poets

the next time the phone rings
it will be a poet.
the next person at the door

will be a poet.
this one teaches
and that one lives with his mother
and that one is writing the story of
Ezra Pound.
oh, brothers, we are the sickest and the
lowest of the breed.

soul

oh, how worried they are about my
soul!
I get letters
the phone rings . . .
"are you going to be all right?"
they ask.
"I'll be all right," I tell them.
"I've seen so many go down the drain,"
they tell me.
"don't worry about me," I say.

yet, they make me nervous.
I go in and take a shower
come out and squeeze a pimple on my
nose.
then I go into the kitchen and make
a salami and ham sandwich.
I used to live on candy bars.
now I have imported German mustard
for my sandwich. I might be in danger
at that.

the phone keeps ringing and the letters keep
arriving.

if you live in a closet with rats and
eat dry bread
they like you.
you're a genius
then.

or if you're in the madhouse or
the drunktank
they call you a genius.

or if you're drunk and shouting
obscenities and
vomiting your life-guts on
the floor
you're a genius.

but get the rent paid up a month in
advance
put on a new pair of stockings
go to the dentist
make love to a healthy clean girl
instead of a whore
and you've lost your
soul.

I'm not interested enough to ask about
their souls.
I suppose I
should.

a change of habit

Shirley came to town with a broken leg
and met the Chicano who smoked
long slim cigars
and they got a place together
on Beacon street
5th floor;
the leg didn't get in the way
too much and
they watched television together
and Shirley cooked, on her
crutches and all;
there was a cat, Bogey,
and they had some friends
and talked about sports and Richard Nixon
and how the hell to
make it.
it worked for some months,
Shirley even got the cast off,
and the Chicano, Manuel,
got a job at the Biltmore,
Shirley sewed all the buttons back on
Manuel's shirts, mended and matched his
socks, then
one day Manuel returned to the place, and
she was gone—
no argument, no note, just
gone, all her clothes
all her stuff, and
Manuel sat by the window and looked out
and didn't make his job
the next day or the
next day or
the day after, he
didn't phone in, he
lost his job, got a

ticket for parking, smoked
four hundred and sixty cigarettes, got
picked up for common drunk, bailed
out, went
to court and pleaded
guilty.

when the rent was up he
moved from Beacon street, he
left the cat and went to live with
his brother and
they'd get drunk
every night
and talk about how
                    terrible
life was.

Manuel never again smoked
long slim cigars
because Shirley always said
how
handsome he looked
when he did.

$$$$$

I've always had trouble with
money.
this one place I worked
everybody ate hot dogs
and potato chips
in the company cafeteria for
3 days before each
payday.
I wanted steaks,
I even went to see the manager
of the cafeteria and
demanded that he serve
steaks. he refused.

I'd forget payday.
I had a high rate of absenteeism and
payday would arrive and everybody would
start talking about
it.
"payday?" I'd say, "hell, is this
payday? I forgot to pick up my
last check . . ."

"stop the bullshit, man . . ."

"no, no, I mean it . . ."

I'd jump up and go down to payroll
and sure enough there'd be a
check and I'd come back and show it
to them. "Jesus Christ, I forgot all about
it . . ."

for some reason they'd get
angry. then the payroll clerk would come

around. I'd have two
checks. "Jesus," I'd say, "two checks."
and they were
angry.
some of them were working
two jobs.

the worst day
it was raining very hard,
I didn't have a raincoat so
I put on a very old coat I hadn't worn for
months and
I walked in a little late
while they were working.
I looked in the coat for some
cigarettes
and found a 5 dollar bill
in the side pocket:
"hey, look," I said, "I just found a 5 dollar
bill I didn't know I had, that's
funny."

"hey, man, knock off the
shit!"

"no, no, I'm *serious*, really, I remember
wearing this coat when
I got drunk at the
bars. I've been rolled too often,
I've got this fear . . . I take money out of
my wallet and hide it all
over me."

"sit down and get to
work."

I reached into an inside pocket:
"hey, look, here's a TWENTY! God, here's a
TWENTY I never knew I

had! I'm
RICH!"

"you're not funny, son of
a bitch . . ."

"hey, my God, here's ANOTHER
twenty! too much, too too
much . . . I *knew* I didn't spend all that
money that night. I thought I'd been
rolled again . . ."

I kept searching the
coat. "hey! here's a ten and
here's a fiver! my God . . ."

"listen, I'm telling you to *sit down
and shut up* . . ."

"my God, I'm RICH . . . I don't even *need*
this job . . ."

"man, sit *down* . . ."

I found another ten after I sat down
but I didn't say
anything.
I could feel waves of hatred and
I was confused,
they believed I had
plotted the whole thing
just to make them
feel bad. I didn't want
to. people who live on hot dogs and
potato chips for
3 days before payday
feel bad
enough.

I sat down
leaned forward and
began to go to
work.

outside
it continued to
rain.

my daughter is most
glorious.
we are eating a take-
out snack in my car
in Santa Monica.
I say, "hey, kid,
my life has been
good, so good."
she looks at me.
I put my head down
on the steering wheel,
shudder, then I
kick the door open,
put on a
mock-puke.
I straighten up.
she laughs
biting into her
sandwich.
I pick up four
french fries
put them into my mouth,
chew them.
it's 5:30 p.m.
and the cars run up
and down past us.
I sneak a look:
we've got all the
luck we need:
her eyes are brilliant with the
remainder of the
day, and she's
grinning.

doom and siesta time

my friend is worried about dying

he lives in Frisco
I live in L.A.

he goes to the gym and
works with the iron and hits
the big bag.

old age diminishes him.

he can't drink because of
his liver.

he can do
50 pushups.

he writes me
letters
telling me
that I'm the only one
who listens to him.

sure, Hal, I answer him
on a postcard.

but I don't want to pay
all those gym fees.

I go to bed
with a liverwurst and
onion sandwich at
one p.m.

after I eat I
nap

with the heli-
copters and vultures
circling over my
sagging mattress.

as crazy as I ever was

drunk and writing poems
at 3 a.m.

what counts now
is one more
tight
pussy

before the light
tilts out

drunk and writing poems
at 3:15 a.m.

some people tell me that I'm
famous.

what am I doing alone
drunk and writing poems at
3:18 a.m.?

I'm as crazy as I ever was
they don't understand
that I haven't stopped hanging out of 4th floor
windows by my heels—
I still do
right now
sitting here

writing this down
I am hanging by my heels
floors up:
68, 72, 101,
the feeling is the
same:

relentless
unheroic and
necessary

sitting here
drunk and writing poems
at 3:24 a.m.

sex

I am driving down Wilton Avenue
when this girl of about 15
dressed in tight blue jeans
that grip her behind like two hands
steps out in front of my car
I stop to let her cross the street
and as I watch her contours waving
she looks directly through my windshield
at me
with purple eyes
and then blows
out of her mouth
the largest pink globe of
bubble gum
I have ever seen
while I am listening to Beethoven
on the car radio.
she enters a small grocery store
and is gone
and I am left with
Ludwig.

dead now

I always wanted to ball
Henry Miller, she said,
but by the time I got there
it was too late.

damn it, I said, you girls
always arrive too late.
I've already masturbated
twice today.

that wasn't his problem,
she said. by the way,
how come you flog-off
so much?

it's the space, I said,
all that space between
poems and stories, it's
intolerable.

you should wait, she said,
you're impatient.

what do you think of Celine?
I asked.

I wanted to ball him too.

dead now, I said.

dead now, she said.

care to hear a little
music? I asked.

might as well, she said.

I gave her Ives.

that's all I had left
that night.

twins

hey, said my friend, I want you to meet
Hangdog Harry, he reminds me of you,
and I said, all right, and we went to
this cheap hotel.
old men sitting around watching
some program on the tv in the lobby
as we went up the stairway
to 209 and there was Hangdog
sitting in a straight strawback chair
bottle of wine at his feet
last year's calendar on the wall,
"you guys sit down," he said,
"that's the problem:
man's inhumanity to man."
we watched him slowly roll a
Bull Durham cigarette.
"I've got a 17 inch neck and I'll kill
anybody who fucks with me."
he licked his cigarette
then spit on the rug.
"just like home here. feel free."

"how you feeling, Hangdog?" asked
my friend.

"terrible. I'm in love with a whore,
haven't seen her in 3 or 4 weeks."

"what you think she's doing, Hang?"

"well, right now about now I'd say
she's sucking some turkeyneck."

he picked up his wine bottle
took a tremendous drain.

"look," my friend said to Hangdog,
"we've got to get going."

"o.k., time and tide, they don't
wait . . ."

he looked at me:
"whatcha say your name was?"

"Salomski."

"pleased to meet cha, kid."

"likewise."

we went down the stairway
they were still in the lobby
looking at t.v.

"what did you think of him?"
my friend asked.

"shit," I said, "he was really
all right. yes."

the place didn't look
bad

she had huge thighs
and a very good laugh
she laughed at everything
and the curtains were yellow
and I finished
rolled off
and before she went to the bathroom
she reached under the bed and
threw me a rag.
it was hard
it was stiff with other men's
sperm.
I wiped off on the sheet.

when she came out
she bent over
and I saw all that behind
as she put Mozart
on.

the little girls

up in northern California
he stood in the pulpit
and had been reading for some time
he had been reading poems about
nature and the goodness
of man.

he knew that everything was all
right and you couldn't blame him:
he was a professor and had never
been in jail or in a whorehouse
had never had a used car die
in a traffic jam;
had never needed more than
3 drinks during his wildest
evening;
had never been rolled, flogged,
mugged,
had never been bitten by a dog
he got nice letters from Gary
Snyder, and his face was
kindly, unmarked and
tender.
his wife had never betrayed him,
nor had his luck.

he said, "I'm just going to read
3 more poems and then I'm going
to step down and let
Bukowski read."

"oh no, William," said all the
little girls in their pink and blue
and white and orange and lavender
dresses, "oh no, William,

read some more, read some
more!"

he read one more poem and then he said,
"this will be the last poem that
I will read."

"oh no, William," said all the little
girls in their red and green see-
through dresses, "oh no, William," said
all the little girls in their tight blue
jeans with little hearts sewn on them,
"oh no, William," said all the little girls,
"read more poems, read more poems!"

but he was good to his word.
he got the poem out and he climbed down and
vanished. as I got up to read
the little girls wiggled in
their seats and some of them hissed and
some of them made remarks to me
which I will use at some later date.

two or three weeks later
I got a letter from William
saying that he *did* enjoy my reading.
a true gentleman.
I was in bed in my underwear with a
3 day hangover. I lost the envelope
but I took the letter and folded it
into a paper airplane such as
I had learned to make in grammar
school. it sailed about the room
before landing between an old Racing Form
and a pair of shit-stained shorts.

we have not corresponded since.

rain or shine

the vultures at the zoo
(all 3 of them)
sit very quietly in their
caged tree
and below
on the ground
are chunks of rotting meat.
the vultures are over-full.
our taxes have fed them
well.

we move on to the next
cage.
a man is in there
sitting on the ground
eating
his own shit.
I recognize him as
our former mailman.
his favorite expression
had been:
"have a beautiful day."

that day, I did.

cold plums

eating cold plums in bed
she told me about the German
who owned everything on the block
except the custom drapery shop
and he tried to buy
the custom drapery shop
but the girls said, no.
the German had the best grocery store in
Pasadena, his meats were high
but worth the price
and his vegetables and produce were
very cheap and
he also sold flowers. people came
from all over Pasadena to go to his
store
but he wanted to buy the custom drapery shop
and the girls kept saying, no.
one night somebody was seen running
out the back door of the drapery shop
and there was a fire
and almost everything was destroyed—
they'd had a tremendous inventory,
they tried to save what was left
had a fire sale
but it didn't work
they had to sell, finally,
and then the German owned the drapery shop
but it just sits there, vacant,
the German's wife tried to make a go of it
she tried to sell little baskets and things
but it didn't work.

we finished the plums.
"that was a sad story," I told her.
then she bent down and began sucking me off.

the windows were open and you could hear me
hollering all over the neighborhood
at 5:30 in the evening.

girls coming home

the girls are coming home in their cars
and I sit by the window and
watch.

there's a girl in a red dress
driving a white car
there's a girl in a blue dress
driving a blue car
there's a girl in a pink dress
driving a red car.

as the girl in the red dress
gets out of the white car
I look at her legs

as the girl in the blue dress
gets out of the blue car
I look at her legs
as the girl in the pink dress
gets out of the red car
I look at her legs.

the girl in the red dress
who got out of the white car
had the best legs

the girl in the pink dress
who got out of the red car
had average legs

but I keep remembering the girl in the blue dress
who got out of the blue car

I saw her panties

you don't know how exciting life can get
around here
at 5:35 p.m.

some picnic

which reminds me
I shacked with Jane for 7 years
she was a drunk
I loved her

my parents hated her
I hated my parents
we made a nice
foursome

one day we went on a picnic
together
up in the hills
and we played cards and drank beer and
ate potato salad

they treated her as if she were a living person
at last

everybody laughed
I didn't laugh.

later at my place
over the whiskey
I said to her,
I don't like them
but it's good they treated you
nice.

you damn fool, she said,
don't you see?

see what?

they kept looking at my beer-belly,

they think I'm pregnant.

oh, I said, well here's to our beautiful
child.

here's to our beautiful child,
she said.

we drank them down.

bedpans

in the hospitals I've been in
you see the crosses on the walls
with the thin palm leaves behind them
yellowed and browned

it is the signal to accept the inevitable

but what really hurts
are the bedpans
hard under your ass
you're dying
and you're supposed to sit up on this
impossible thing
and urinate and
defecate

while in the bed
next to yours
a family of 5 brings good cheer
to an incurable
heart-case
cancer-case
or a case of general rot.

the bedpan is a merciless rock
a horrible mockery
because nobody wants to drag your failing body
to the crapper and back.

you'd drag it
but they've got the bars up:
you're in your crib
your tiny death-crib
and when the nurse comes back
an hour and a half later

and there's nothing in the bedpan
she gives you a most
intemperate look

as if when nearing death
one should be able to do
the common common things
again and again.

but if you think that's bad
just relax
and let it go
all of it
into the sheets

then you'll hear it
not only from the nurse
but from
all the other patients . . .

the hardest part of dying
is that they expect you
to go out
like a rocket shot into the
night sky.

sometimes that can be done

but when you need the bullet and the gun
you'll look up
and find
that the wires above your head
connected to the button
years ago
have been cut
snipped
eliminated
been

made
useless as
the bedpan.

the good loser

red face
Texas
and age
he's at an L.A.
racetrack
been talking to
a group of folks.
it's the 4th race
and he's ready to
leave:
"well, goodbye,
folks and God bless,
see you around
tomorrow . . ."

"nice fellow."
"yeh."

he's going to the
parking lot to
get into a 12 year
old car

from there he'll
drive to a roominghouse

his room will neither
have a toilet nor a
bath

his room will have
one window with a
torn paper shade
and outside will be

a crumbling cement wall
spray-can graffiti courtesy
of a Chicano youth gang

he'll take off his
shoes and
get on the bed

it will be dark
but he won't turn
on the light

he's got nothing
to do.

an art

all the way from Mexico
straight from the fields
to 14 wins
13 by k.o.
he was ranked #3
and in a tune-up fight
he was k.o'd by an unranked
black fighter who hadn't fought
in 2 years.

all the way from Mexico
straight from the fields
the drink and the women had gotten
to him.
in the rematch he was k.o'd again
and suspended for 6 months.

all that way
for the bottle and 2 cases of
v.d.

he came back in a year
swearing he was clean, he'd
learned.
and he earned a draw with the
9th ranked in his division.

he came back for the rematch
and the fight was stopped in
the 3rd round because he
couldn't protect
himself.

and he went all the way back
to Mexico
straight to the fields.

it takes a damned good poet
like me
to handle drink and women
evade v.d.
write about failures
like him
and hold my ranking in the
top 10:
all the way from Germany
straight from the factories
among beerbottles
and the ringing of the
phone.

the girls at the green
hotel

are more beautiful than
movie stars
and they lounge on the
lawn
sunbathing
and one sits in a short
dress and high
heels, legs crossed
exposing miraculous
thighs.
she has a bandanna
on her head
and smokes a
long cigarette.
traffic slows
almost stops.

the girls ignore
the traffic.
they are half
asleep in the afternoon
they are whores
they are whores without
souls
and they are magic
because they lie
about nothing.

I get in my car
wait for traffic to
clear,
drive across the street
to the green hotel
to my favorite:

276

she is
sun-bathing on the
lawn nearest the
curb.

"hello," I say.
she turns eyes like
imitation diamonds
up at me.
her face has no
expression.

I drop my latest
book of poems
out the car
window.
it falls
by her side.

I shift into
low,
drive off.

there'll be some
laughs
tonight.

a good one

I get too many
phone calls.
they seek the
creature out.
they shouldn't.

I never phoned
Knut Hamsun or
Ernie or
Celine.

I never phoned
Salinger
I never phoned
Neruda.

tonight I got
a call:

"hello. you
Charles Bukowski?"

"yes."

"well, I got a
house."

"yes?"

"a bordello."

"I understand."

"I've read your
books. I've got a

houseboat in
Sausalito."

"all right."

"I want to give you
my phone number. you
ever come to San Francisco
I'll buy you a drink."

"o.k. give me the
number."

I took it down.

"we run a class joint. we're
after lawyers and state senators,
upper class citizens, muggers,
pimps, the like."

"I'll phone you when I
get up there."

"lots of the girls
read your books. they
love you."

"yeah?"
"yeah."

we said goodbye.

I liked that
phone call.

shit time

half drunk
I left her place
her warm blankets
and I was hungover
didn't even know what town
it was.
I walked along and
I couldn't find my car.
but I knew it was somewhere.
and then I was lost
too.
I walked around. it was a
Wednesday morning and I could
see the ocean to the south.
but all that drinking:
the shit was about to pour
out of me.
I walked towards the
sea.
I saw a brown brick
structure at the edge
of the sea.
I walked in. there was an
old guy groaning on one of
the pots.
"hi, buddy," he said.
"hi," I said.
"it's hell out there,
isn't it?" the old guy
asked.
"it is," I answered.
"need a drink?"
"never before noon."
"what time you got?"
"11:58."
"we got two minutes."

I wiped, flushed, pulled up my
pants and walked over.
the old man was still on his pot,
groaning.
he pointed to a bottle of wine
at his feet
it was almost done
and I picked it up and took about
half what remained.
I handed him a very old and wrinkled
dollar
then walked outside on the lawn
and puked it up.
I looked at the ocean and the
ocean looked good, full of blues and
greens and sharks.
I walked back out of there
and down the street
determined to find my automobile.
it took me one hour and 15 minutes
and when I found it
I got in and drove off
pretending that I knew just as much
as the next
man.

madness

I don't beat the walls with my fists
I just sit
but it rushes in
a tide of it.

the woman in the court behind me howls,
weeps every night.
sometimes the county comes
and takes her away for a day or two.

I believed she was suffering the loss
of a great love
until one day she came over and told me about
it—
she had lost 8 apartment houses
to a gigolo who had swindled her out
of them.
she was howling and weeping over loss of property.
she began weeping as she told me
then with a mouth lined with stale lipstick
and smelling of garlic and onions
she kissed me and told me:
"Hank, nobody loves you if you don't have money."

she's old, almost as old as I am.

she left, still weeping . . .

the other morning at 7:30 a.m. two black
attendants came with their stretcher,
only they knocked on my door.

"come on, man," said the tallest
one.

"wait," I said, "there's a mistake."

I was terribly hungover
standing in my torn bathrobe
hair hanging down over my eyes.

"this is the address they gave us, man,
this is 5437 and 2/5's isn't it?"

"yes."

"come on, man, don't give us no shit."

"the lady you want is in the back there."

they both walked around back.

"this door here?"

"no, no, that's my back door. look go up those steps behind
you there. it's the door to the east, the one with the mailbox
hanging loose."

they went up and banged on the door. I watched them take her
away. they didn't use the stretcher. she walked between them.
and the thought occurred to me that they were taking the wrong
one but I wasn't sure.

a 56 year old poem

I went with two ladies
down to Venice
to look for antique furniture.
I parked in back of the store
and went in with them.
$125 for a clock, $700 for 6 chairs.
I stopped looking.

the ladies moved around
looking at everything.
the ladies had class.
I waved goodbye to one of the ladies
and walked out.

it was Sunday and the bar
wasn't much better,
everybody was nervous and young
and blonde and pale.
I finished my drink, got 4 beers
at the liquor store
and sat in my car drinking them.

finishing the 4th beer
the ladies came out.
they asked me if I was all right.
I told them that every experience
meant something
and that they had pulled me out of
my usual murky
current.

the one I knew best had bought a table
with a marble top for $100.
she owned her own business and was a
civilized person.

she was civilized enough to know a neighbor
who had a van
and while I sat in her apartment drinking
1974 *Zeller Schwarze Katz*
they went down and got the table.

later she wanted to know what I thought about
the table and I said I thought it was all right,
sometimes I lost one hundred dollars at the
racetrack. we watched tv in bed and later
that night I couldn't come. I think it was
because I was thinking about that marble table.
I'm sure it was. I don't have any antique marble
tables at my place, I almost never have any sex trouble at
my place. sometimes but
very seldom.
I don't understand the whole antique
business

I'm sure it's a giant
con.

the beautiful young girl
walking past the graveyard—

I stop my car at the signal
I see her walking past the graveyard—

as she walks past the iron fence
I can see through the iron fence
and I see the headstones
and the green lawn.

her body moves in front of the iron fence
the headstones do not move.

I think,
doesn't anybody else see this?

I think,
does she see those headstones?

if she does
she has wisdom that I don't have
for she appears to ignore them.

her body moving in its
magic fluid
and her long hair is lighted
by the 3 p.m. sun.

the signal changes
she crosses the street to the west
I drive west.

I drive my car down to the ocean
get out
and run up and down
in front of the sea for 35 minutes

seeing people here and there
with eyes and ears and toes
and various other parts.

nobody seems to care.

beer

I don't know how many bottles of beer
I have consumed while waiting for things
to get better.
I don't know how much wine and whiskey
and beer
mostly beer
I have consumed after
splits with women—
waiting for the phone to ring
waiting for the sound of footsteps,
and the phone never rings
until much later
and the footsteps never arrive
until much later.
when my stomach is coming up
out of my mouth
they arrive as fresh as spring flowers:
"what the hell have you done to yourself?
it will be 3 days before you can fuck me!"

the female is durable
she lives seven and one half years longer
than the male, and she drinks very little beer
because she knows it's bad for the
figure.

while we are going mad
they are out
dancing and laughing
with horny cowboys.

well, there's beer
sacks and sacks of empty beer bottles
and when you pick one up
the bottles fall through the wet bottom

of the paper sack
rolling
clanking
spilling grey wet ash
and stale beer,
or the sacks fall over at 4 a.m.
in the morning
making the only sound in your life.

beer
rivers and seas of beer
beer beer beer
the radio singing love songs
as the phone remains silent
and the walls stand
straight up and down
and beer is all there is.

artist

all of a sudden I'm a painter.
a girl from Galveston gives me
$50 for a painting of a man
holding a candycane while
floating in a darkened sky.

than a young man with a black beard
comes over
and I sell him three for $80.
he likes rugged stuff
where I write across the painting—
"shoot shit" or "GRATE ART IS
HORSESHIT, BUY TACOS."

I can do a painting in 5 minutes.
I use acrylics, paint right out of
the tube.
I do the left side of the painting
first with my left hand and then
finish the right side with my
right hand.

now the man with the black beard
comes back with a friend whose hair
sticks out and they have a young blonde
girl with them.

black beard is still a sucker:
I sell him a hunk of shit—
an orange dog with the word
"DOG" written on his side.

stick-out hair wants 3 paintings
for which I ask $70.
he doesn't have the money.

I keep the paintings but
he promises to send me a
girl called Judy
in garter belt and high heels.
he's already told her about me:
"a world-renowned writer," he said
and she said, "oh no!" and pulled
her dress up over her head.
"I want that," I told him.

then we haggled over terms
I wanted to fuck her first
then get head later.
"how about head first and
fuck later?" he asked.

"that doesn't work," I
said.

so we agreed:
Judy will come by and
afterwards
I will hand her the
3 paintings.
so there we are:
back to the barter system,
the only way to beat
inflation.

never the less,
I'd like to
start the Men's Liberation Movement:
I want a woman to hand *me* 3 of her
paintings after I have
made love to her,
and if she can't paint
she can leave me
a couple of golden earrings
or maybe a slice of ear
in memory of one who
could.

my old man

16 years old
during the depression
I'd come home drunk
and all my clothing—
shorts, shirts, stockings—
suitcase, and pages of
short stories
would be thrown out on the
front lawn and about the
street.

my mother would be
waiting behind a tree:
"Henry, Henry, don't
go in . . . he'll
kill you, he's read
your stories . . ."

"I can whip his
ass . . ."

"Henry, please take
this . . . and
find yourself a room."

but it worried him
that I might not
finish high school
so I'd be back
again.

one evening he walked in
with the pages of
one of my short stories
(which I had never submitted

to him)
and he said, "this is
a great short story."
I said, "o.k.,"
and he handed it to me
and I read it.
it was a story about
a rich man
who had a fight with
his wife and had
gone out into the night
for a cup of coffee
and had observed
the waitress and the spoons
and forks and the
salt and pepper shakers
and the neon sign
in the window
and then had gone back
to his stable
to see and touch his
favorite horse
who then
kicked him in the head
and killed him.

somehow
the story held
meaning for him
though
when I had written it
I had no idea
of what I was
writing about.

so I told him,
"o.k., old man, you can
have it."

and he took it
and walked out
and closed the door.
I guess that's
as close
as we ever got.

fear

he walks up to my Volks
after I have parked
and rocks it back and
forth
grinning around his
cigar.

"hey, Hank, I notice
all the women around your
place lately . . . good looking
stuff; you're doing all
right."

"Sam," I say, "that's not
true; I am one of God's most
lonely men."

"we got some nice girls at
the parlor, you oughta try
some of them."

"I'm afraid of those places,
Sam, I can't walk into them."

"I'll send you a girl then,
real nice stuff."

"Sam, don't send me a whore,
I always fall in love with
whores."

"o.k., friend," he says,
"let me know if you change
your mind."

I watch him walk away.
some men are always on
top of their game.
I am mostly always
confused.

he can break a man
in half
and doesn't know who
Mozart is.

who wants to listen
to music
anyhow
on a rainy Wednesday
night?

little tigers everywhere

Sam the whorehouse man
has squeaky shoes
and he walks up and down
the court
squeaking and talking to
the cats.
he's 310 pounds,
a killer
and he talks to the cats.
he sees the women at the massage
parlor and has no girlfriends
no automobile
he doesn't drink or dope
his biggest vices are
chewing on a cigar and
feeding all the cats in
the neighborhood.
some of the cats get
pregnant
and so finally there are
more and more cats and
everytime I open my door
one or two cats will
run in and sometimes I'll
forget they are there and
they'll shit under the bed
or I'll awaken at night
hearing sounds
leap up with my blade
sneak into the kitchen and
find one of Sam the whorehouse
man's cats walking around on
the sink or sitting on top
of the refrigerator.

Sam runs the love parlor
around the corner
and his girls stand in the
doorway in the sun
and the traffic signals go
red and green and red and green
and all of Sam's cats
possess some of the meaning
as do the days and the nights.

after the reading:

". . . I've seen people in front of
their typewriters in such a bind
that it would blow their intestines
right out of their assholes if they
were trying to shit."

"ah hahaha hahaha!"

". . . it's a shame to work *that*
hard to try to write."

"ah hahaha hahaha!"

"ambition rarely has anything to
do with talent. luck is best, and
talent limps along a little
bit behind luck."

"ah haha."

he rose and left with an 18 year old virgin, the most
beautiful co-ed of them
all.
I closed my notebook
got up and limped a
little bit behind
them.

about cranes

sometimes after you get your ass
kicked real good by the forces

you often wish you were a crane
standing on one leg

in blue water

but there's
the
old up-bringing
you know:

you don't want to be
a crane
standing on one leg

in blue water

the distress is not
enough

and

the victory
limps

a crane can't
buy a piece of ass

or

hang itself at noon
in Monterey

those are some of
the things

humans can do

besides
stand on one leg

a gold pocket watch

my grandfather was a tall German
with a strange smell on his breath.
he stood very straight
in front of his small house
and his wife hated him
and his children thought him odd.
I was six the first time we met
and he gave me all his war medals.
the second time I met him
he gave me his gold pocket watch.
it was very heavy and I took it home
and wound it very tight
and it stopped running
which made me feel bad.
I never saw him again
and my parents never spoke of him
nor did my grandmother
who had long ago
stopped living with him.
once I asked about him
and they told me
he drank too much
but I liked him best
standing very straight
in front of his house
and saying, "hello, Henry, you
and I, we know each
other."

beach trip

the strong men
the muscle men
there they sit
down at the beach
cocoa tans
with the weights
scattered about them
untouched

they sit as the
waves go in and
out

they sit as the
stock market
makes and breaks
men and families

they sit while
one punch of a button
could turn their
turkeynecks to
black and shriveled
matchsticks

they sit while
suicides in green rooms
trade it in for space

they sit while former
Miss Americas
weep before wrinkled
mirrors

they sit

they sit with less
life-flow than apes
and my woman stops and
looks at them:
"oooh oooh oooh," she
says.

I walk off with
my woman as the waves
go in and out.

"there's something wrong
with them," she said, "what
is it?"

"their love only runs in
one direction."

the seagulls whirl and
the sea runs in and out

and we left them
back there
wasting themselves
time
this moment
the seagulls
the sea
the sand.

one for the shoeshine man

the balance is preserved by the snails climbing the
Santa Monica cliffs;
the luck is in walking down Western Avenue
and having the girls in a massage
parlor holler at you, "Hello, Sweetie!"
the miracle is having 5 women in love
with you at the age of 55,
and the goodness is that you are only able
to love one of them.
the gift is having a daughter more gentle
than you are, whose laughter is finer
than yours.
the peace comes from driving a
blue 67 Volks through the streets like a
teenager, radio tuned to The Host Who Loves You
Most, feeling the sun, feeling the solid hum
of the rebuilt motor
as you needle through traffic.
the grace is being able to like rock music,
symphony music, jazz . . .
anything that contains the original energy of
joy.

and the probability that returns
is the deep blue low
yourself flat upon yourself
within the guillotine walls
angry at the sound of the phone
or anybody's footsteps passing;
but the other probability—
the lilting high that always follows—
makes the girl at the checkstand in the
supermarket look like
Marilyn
like Jackie before they got her Harvard lover

like the girl in high school that we
all followed home.

there is that which helps you believe
in something else besides death:
somebody in a car approaching
on a street too narrow,
and he or she pulls aside to let you
by, or the old fighter Beau Jack
shining shoes
after blowing the entire bankroll
on parties
on women
on parasites,
humming, breathing on the leather,
working the rag
looking up and saying:
"what the hell, I had it for a
while. that beats the
other."

I am bitter sometimes
but the taste has often been
sweet. it's only that I've
feared to say it. it's like
when your woman says,
"tell me you love me," and
you can't.

if you see me grinning from
my blue Volks
running a yellow light
driving straight into the sun
I will be locked in the
arms of a
crazy life
thinking of trapeze artists
of midgets with big cigars
of a Russian winter in the early 40's
of Chopin with his bag of Polish soil

of an old waitress bringing me an extra
cup of coffee and laughing
as she does so.

the best of you
I like more than you think.
the others don't count
except that they have fingers and heads
and some of them eyes
and most of them legs
and all of them
good and bad dreams
and a way to go.

justice is everywhere and it's working
and the machine guns and the frogs
and the hedges will tell you
so.

Photo: Richard Robinson

A major figure in contemporary American poetry and prose, Charles Bukowski was born in Andernach, Germany in 1920, and brought to the United States at the age of two. He was raised in Los Angeles where he continues to live. He published his first short story when he was twenty-four and began writing poetry at the age of thirty-five. He has now published more than twenty books of poetry and prose, the most recent of which are his Selected Poems 1955-1973: *Burning In Water, Drowning In Flame* (Black Sparrow, 1974) and a novel, *Factotum* (Black Sparrow, 1975). Most of his books have now been published in translation, and his poems and stories continue to appear in magazines and newspapers throughout the world.